The Interim Manager's Guide to Success

Andrew Gordon

PublishNation
www.publishnation.co.uk

When I started to write this book I used the phrases "he or she", "him or her" and "his or hers" to the point at which it became wearisome for me and probably irritating for the reader. So in the end I reverted to just the male pronouns and possessive. I hope my more sensitive readers can find it in their hearts to forgive me.

This book is dedicated to the man who taught me to read, with all my love.

Contents

Introduction

Interim management is a rapidly growing field. In the UK alone it is estimated there are more than 16,000 active interim managers[1]. This can only be a guess but there is no doubt that the numbers of interims are rising. The rise of the interim manager reflects some key trends in UK business:

- Organisational life is increasingly short-termist and driven by change and uncertainty. Organisations are more frequently caught with a gap in the skills of their management team, a gap which needs filling quickly.

- Many organisations, in a drive to stay streamlined and keep costs to a minimum, are unwilling to commit to long-term expense until they are sure that the skills are needed. The salary of a permanent senior employee is a significant expense for any firm and an interim is a good way of getting the skills needed without committing to a long-term employment contract; if the skills prove unnecessary the interim's contract can be terminated without fuss or compensation (outside the contractual notice period).

- In the economies of many of the developed nations full employment has become a reality. Skills are in short-supply. When one manager leaves a firm it can take a great deal of time - a year is not unusual for senior positions - to find his 'permanent' replacement and get him or her on board.

- In the increasingly service-based economies of the developed world the success or failure of many firms depends on the

---

[1] Estimated by the Institute of Interim Management. Their website is an excellent place to start for anyone new to interim management: *https://iim.org.uk/*

knowledge and skills of key individuals. Firms cannot allow posts to go unfilled for too long, or use junior staff to 'cover' for the role; the risk is simply too great.

An interesting phenomenon is that the average age of interim managers is coming down. Not so long ago most interim managers were in their fifties or sixties; people who had achieved financial security but were not ready to give up the fight just yet. These days it is increasingly seen as an option for younger people by individuals who see interim management as a long-term career option in its own right, people with families to raise and mortgages to pay. I started my interim career at the age of 36, which at the time was seen as an odd career move.

In this book I use the phrase 'permanent employee' to differentiate from an interim manager. But is there any such thing these days as a 'permanent' role? Few professional people today expect to work for one employer for the whole of their career. It seems to me that we have all become interims of a kind, shifting from one role and organisation to the next.

This book contains the distilled experience of someone who has made a successful career as an interim manager. I do not for one minute suppose that I am the best interim manager in the world but in an interim career spanning nearly two decades I have made an excellent living[2]. More importantly for you, Dear Reader, I have made and observed a lot of the mistakes that weaker interims make, and learned from them. This book contains advice about the practical, day-to-day issues of succeeding as an interim manager.

---

[2] In a 15-year career (and still going!) I have had 26 discrete engagements with 23 clients. Some of those gigs were pure consultancy but most were proper interim engagements of the kind I describe in this book. The average length of my engagements has been about six months, which is par for the course. An interim career is never going to make you rich - there is a limit to what one can charge and only so many days in a year - but I can't complain. The huge upside for me has been the work-life balance that would never have been possible in a 'permanent' career.

Issues such as finding clients, winning business, negotiating contracts and fee rates, getting started on a client assignment, dealing with client staff; the stuff that when I first became an interim manager I had to find out myself, the hard way. Anyone contemplating a career in interim management will benefit from learning these lessons the easy way; by reading this book.

Interim management is different from consultancy but I am the first to acknowledge that the skills I learned as a young management consultant working for two of what are often referred to as the 'Big Four' consultancy firms have stood me in good stead. A successful interim needs some of the skills a good consultant regularly uses. So I have written this book to give anyone contemplating interim work but who does not have consultancy experience an insight into the tricks of the trade. They are not difficult skills to learn but they will make a huge difference to your success.

What you won't find in this book is any management theory. There is no mention of any management fad of the last twenty years. Nor will you find any quotes from Machiavelli, Jack Welch (whose ideas are about as far removed from my own as you can get), Tom Peters or any other management 'guru'. I assume that you have already proved yourself as a people manager. Where I talk about the special problems associated with managing people during an interim assignment my advice is based on what I hope is the kind of common-sense practical experience anyone can understand, written in plain, jargon-free English.

In other words, I have simply written the book I wish I had read before I embarked on my interim career.

About the author

Andrew Gordon is an Interim Manager and self-employed consultant specialising in Compliance, Internal Audit and Risk Management for the financial services industry (with occasional and very welcome forays into the real world that actually makes things). He worked for six years as a consultant for two of the 'Big Four' consultancy firms and has 15 years' experience as a freelance consultant and interim, dating from his first assignment aged 36.

What attracts people to interim management?

Here are some of the advantages of interim management compared to permanent employment:

- Variety: As an interim you will be exposed to a wide range of client firms, business types, people, systems and processes. Some interims are able to find work across different industries and different countries.

- Career advancement: This can work both ways but interim management can be a great way of packing a lot of career experience into a short time and developing yourself in the process. Some interims who go back into permanent roles find that their interim experiences have accelerated their climb up the corporate ladder. On the other hand interims can often find themselves working one level below their competence (clients like over-qualified people taking on their problems) which is not conducive to career progression. Assignments are not always stretching, and can even become rather repetitious, depending on how easily you are able to find variety in your assignments.

- Control: As an interim you are in charge of the direction of your career in a way which is difficult to achieve as a permanent employee. It allows you much more scope to fit your working life into your non-working life is a way which suits you, and to achieve the 'work/life balance' that so many organisations talk about but rarely succeed at creating.

- Flexibility: As an interim you can take much more holiday time than the paltry 25 days or so that is the average lot of the permanent employee. Sometimes this holiday is forced; in the downtime between client assignments an interim is on 'holiday' in the same way that an actor is 'resting' between roles. But a successful interim can to some extent control his downtime and take holiday when it suits him, for as long as it suits him, client demands permitting. Some interims also use it as a way of achieving part-time working arrangements, although as I discuss later in this book this is not always easy.

- Money: Let's make no bones about it, successful interim managers earn more, often substantially more, than their skills would command in the world of permanent employment. Interims in work often charge fee rates twice to three times their previous salary. But of course this depends on how successful you are at finding interim assignments; an unsuccessful interim is simply unemployed - but that's why you're reading this book! There can also be some tax advantages to being self-employed but in my experience these are negligible and should not sway any decision to become an interim.

- Challenge: Interim management is not for the faint-hearted. Interims are often used to fill unappealing roles, or to deal with situations where a previous incumbent has failed and left an unholy mess to clear up. Interims are often given difficult objectives and short timescales in which to achieve them. Client employees can be untrusting, openly hostile, or covertly disruptive. People who relish this kind of thing see interim management as a way of getting plenty of it.

What are the downsides of interim management?

The biggest issues are:

- Lack of security: An interim's job security is the notice period on his current assignment contract; normally one to three months. One could argue that the so-called 'security' that goes with permanent employment is no more substantial than the security offered to an interim but the reality is that as an employee, in the UK at least, if your performance is not up to scratch your employer is obliged to give you time, support and training to achieve the competence required, and will continue to pay your salary and benefits during that period. (The alternative is that the employer pays you off under what is known as a "compromise agreement"; these are often quite generous.) As an interim, if your performance doesn't meet the client firm's requirements, you know where the door is…

- Lack of career advancement: As an interim it is possible to find yourself just as much in a rut as a permanent employee; there is no career advancement if you go from one interim role to another similar role. You need to be a "safe pair of hands" and so the 'Peter Principle' applies in reverse; your career can plateau at one level below your competence. Whilst this helps in keeping your stress levels down, and helps to guarantee successful assignments, it can be depressing for anyone whose spark of ambition is still glowing. So if you feel you still have some way to climb up the greasy pole maybe you should postpone the switch to interim management for a while.

- Travel: As an interim you have to go where the work is. This can sometimes mean long commutes, and days or weeks spent away from home. And client firms can be less than generous about travel and hotel expenses incurred by interims. Why should they care? - you're only a contractor, after all.

- Salesmanship: As an employee the only time you normally find yourself having to sell yourself and your skills is when you are being considered for promotion - and sometimes not even then. As an interim you have to go through this selling exercise every time you try to win a client or extend an assignment. And if you don't get a sale you don't eat; not a risk for an employee simply seeking a better job.

- As discussed above, it isn't a career for someone who needs warm, mutually supportive relationships with colleagues they have known for some time and who are friends outside work. An interim can of course enjoy excellent relationships with his client colleagues - in fact his career success depends on his ability to get on with people and command respect - but at the

9

end of the assignment an interim is going to move on. For some, this is hard.

- Getting paid: As an employee it is unlikely (although I accept not impossible) that your employer will go suddenly bust and be unable to pay last month's salary. As an interim this risk is much more real; contracted suppliers are last in line for payment when a firm goes belly-up. How important this risk is to you will of course depend on the line of work you are in and the kind of clients for whom you work but you should bear in mind that if you are contracting via an agency it is the risk of the agency going bust that should worry you; the solvency of the client is neither here nor there. And agencies do go bust from time to time!

If you are the kind of person who enjoys the big desk in the plush corner office, the allocated car parking space, business-class flights, and a dedicated PA who hangs on your every word, then interim management is not for you. As an interim you get what you are given in this regard, and I am used to having to park in the multi-storey three blocks away and work from a wobbly desk near the door to the toilets. If my client provides a PA I am normally at a loss as to how to keep her (and they have all been female) fully occupied; I have grown so self-reliant over the years that I find it difficult to keep her busy. (My usual approach when given a PA is to share her time with the rest of the department, and to develop her as a fully-fledged member of the department rather than just as a PA.) So far as plush offices are concerned, I find myself uncomfortable even when allocated one, and my advice to other interim managers is to decline them whenever possible. I've managed departments of over 200 people without ever feeling the need for an office.

In fact the bigger my department the less inclined I am to hide myself away from the action. As a newcomer to the organisation you will need to quickly build a relationship with your colleagues and shutting yourself away in a box isn't conducive to that. When I am allocated an office I normally suggest that it be used as a meeting room (meeting rooms always seem to be in desperately short-supply in any organisation) and I set up a desk in the middle of the floor. That way I can see and hear what's going on, which I find essential in order to find out what I need to know. And taking a desk next to everyone else makes me accessible and approachable, again essential if I am to achieve the changes I need to achieve.

Still interested?

So you think you're good enough?

After umpteen years in the business you think you have the kind of knowledge, skills and experience that firms (other than your current employer) are going to be prepared to pay for on a contract basis. Is your confidence justified?

Probably not. I say this because I have seen a lot of friends and acquaintances make the decision to become self-employed and offer their services as an interim, only to find themselves out of work for too long and forced back into full-time employment. Often they manage to complete just one interim assignment - the one that enticed them out of permanent employment in the first instance - and fail to find a second. Over the years I have seen more new interim managers fail than succeed, so my pessimism is, statistically at least, justified. They fail because they overlook some basic requirements for success:

You must have something for sale that someone really needs to buy

It is not enough to have skills, knowledge and experience in abundance. Someone has got to be prepared to pay serious money (and there is no point in being an interim if you are not being paid serious money) for your talents, and that 'someone' had better be a big enough number of firms and not just your current employer, or your current employer's competitor. You may be God's gift to (say) the world of supply chain management but unless successful supply chain management is critical to the success of those businesses that operate it, and unless there is a steady stream of firms who are short of a supply chain manager or two, and unless supply chain managers are in short supply (no irony intended) you are simply not going to get work as an interim supply chain manager. In other words, you need to proffer your skills in a seller's market.

Successful interims therefore tend to operate in areas where there is significant change going on. They provide advice and support to an industry that is being forced to address fundamental changes in the way they do business, and where there is human traffic, by which I mean firms are losing key individuals to competitors. Industries that operate in a steady, mature environment are less likely to need short-term assistance; any losses of personnel are easy to cope with by moving employees around rather than by approaching an interim, and in any case firms in such an environment are less likely to implement big projects they don't already have internal expertise to lead.

You need to be very, very good

You may think you're good, but that just isn't enough to make you a high-roller in the interim market. You need to be very, very good. There must be no significant gaps in your qualifications, skills and knowledge, and you must be able to offer a complete package within your area of expertise. If you are a one-trick pony you won't last long. It helps to be over-qualified for the roles you are looking for. So, if you are marketing yourself as an interim corporate chicken-sexer or whatever, you need to be the quickest and most accurate chicken-sexer in the business, with hard evidence to prove it, and you probably need to be able to sex goslings and ducklings as well.

Many budding interim managers make the mistake of assuming that because they have proven technical competence they will find a ready buyer for that competence. Yes, I am sure that some people make a very good living by providing purely technical support - this is after all the basis of a huge IT contracting industry - but most interims need to offer more. To go into a business about which you know little or nothing, to be able to get to the bottom of the many problems it has that you are expected to solve, to make your managers and colleagues see things your way and support you, and to solve those problems permanently and in a way that won't require you to be there forever with your finger in the dam, takes more than just technical competence. I discuss the skills you will need in greater detail later in this book but my experience as an interim has shown me that my particular area of technical competence (in which I am the world's leading expert, obviously) is only a small part of what I have needed to survive and thrive as an interim.

You need a thick skin

Being an interim manager is hard way to make a living. Generally you will be going into a business that is facing a big problem; if they weren't, you wouldn't be needed. (This is not always the case but in my experience interims are usually expected to be trouble-shooters, not just caretakers.) You will sometimes find yourself replacing a failed predecessor and inheriting from him a pile of poop. You will often be given a team who won't necessarily be on your side and who will be inclined to see you as a clueless outsider, maybe even as a threat. Some of your colleagues may have fancied the job you now occupy and will be hoping - and perhaps even quietly seeing to it - that you fail.

Dealing with these pressures and achieving the objectives you have been given takes guts and determination. If you are the kind of person who needs lots of love, cuddles and happiness in your working life, interim management is not for you.

Of course, I am deliberately painting a bleak picture, just so you understand what interim management can sometimes be like. To be fair some of the assignments I have enjoyed have been with wonderful clients, working with colleagues who have become firm friends and who have helped me solve some fascinating problems. But other assignments have been far from this; as an interim you have to take the rough with the smooth and play with whatever cards you are dealt. I talk later in this book about the attributes of a good (i.e. financially successful) interim manager but for now let me say that an interim needs the skin of a rhinoceros. If you are a sensitive plant I recommend you put this book down now and try to find alternative routes to career happiness.

What makes a good interim manager?

Be the best at what you do, and make it clear what this is!

As I have already said, you need to be confident that the service you offer is second-to-none. This does not mean that you have to be able to do everything. The point is that if you are selling yourself as (say) an Interim Health & Safety Officer, you have to know all there is to know about Health & Safety, be up to date with the latest legislation, and what's pending, and have the inside track on how other firms are meeting H&S requirements. You need to be able to quickly analyse a firm's H&S issues and exposures, and have the credibility and presentation skills to be able to communicate your findings, and what needs to be done about them, to senior management in a way that gets their commitment to change.

It's about managing your client's expectations: If you claim expertise, make sure the client knows what area you are an expert in, and what areas you are not an expert in.

Having the knowledge to do the job is important in one key respect: It earns you the right to assume a position of command over a department or project team. Yes, it is of course possible to run a team without knowing everything they know but believe me, it is much easier when you can show (without showing off) that *you* have the skills and experience too. You need to earn respect, not just claim it.

You need to be flexible

A fact of life as an interim is that you have to go where the work is. At the start of your interim career at least, and until you have built up a substantial buffer fund that can tide you over in the lean times (see my advice on 'Taking control of your finances' later in this book) you cannot afford to be too precious about what kind of work you do,

14

or who for, or too fussy about how far you are prepared to travel, how many days a week you work, or how many nights you stay over.

Having said this, I know that some interims do manage to work part-time, or restrict themselves to assignments to which they can commute, and sometimes both. There are many family men and women who are attracted to interim management precisely so that they can bring this kind of flexibility into their working lives. It's great if you can achieve this but obviously demanding these kinds of arrangements from potential clients will restrict your ability to win new assignments, and it may damage your fee rate. I also find that if you are operating at a senior level (by this I mean at Board level - or its public sector equivalent - or one level below) this kind of flexibility can be difficult to achieve. A client with a big problem wants you there full-time, five days a week, until the problem has gone away, and it's hard enough to arrange those crucial business meetings when all of the attendees are full-time. If you are a part-timer, it's even harder.

If you are looking for more flexible arrangements one compromise that is sometimes possible is to suggest to the client that you will work four days a week (say) but that you will ensure that business demands determine which day you will take off. So, for example, if you need to attend a meeting on Monday you will work Monday, and take Friday off instead, or vice versa. But even this type of arrangement is more likely to work if you are an interim in charge of a stand-alone project rather than an interim running a department. Managing people on a day-to-day basis is made more difficult by distance and absence, despite today's amazing communications technology.

I often find that my assignments demand my complete and undivided attention for the early part of the contract, and that towards the end, as the problem I have been asked to solve comes under control, I am able to take time off, or spend some time working from home. I manage this as part of my general approach to interim management; by making myself effectively redundant. I do this by making the changes that need to be made, by delegating, by training my colleagues to do what I do, and by coaching my eventual successor. A graduated hand-over process can then be achieved, allowing me to spend time away looking for the next project, or just enjoying myself. I take care to explain to clients that I intend to adopt this approach as a way of ensuring a successful hand-over, and as a way of keeping my fees down; clients usually accept this!

If you are looking for flexible working arrangements as an interim you should also bear in mind that it is harder to achieve change when you are only around some of the time. The more you are on site the more quickly you will detect what needs to be changed, and the more easily will you be able to get into the heads of those people who are causing the problem and whose attitude and behaviours need to be changed. Management is after all defined as getting things done through other people, and as an interim manager you have a limited opportunity to make it happen. Working part-time reduces that opportunity even further.

Another fact of life as an interim is that you have to be flexible about contractual terms. It's great to be offered a solid six-month contract with three months' notice on either side (a notice period of a month is more common) but I have taken work on a week's notice for clients who have made no promises that the assignment will last even that long. Often I agree to work for as long as it takes to replace me with a full-time employee. This normally takes longer than people expect so I am prepared to accept the risk. So long as the money is right, of course!

Nor can you afford to be prissy about the job title you are given, or who you report to. I'm happy to be called whatever the client likes, and report to the most junior or inappropriate person the client can find, so long as my fee gets paid. But the harder the client makes the achievement of my objectives, the higher my fee rate; this is why that early discussion with the client before contracts are signed is so important. There will more, much more, on this vital discussion later in the book.

I tend to be nervous about short-term interim assignments. In most lines of work it takes a good six months work for an individual coming in at any level to have an impact upon an organisation and for that impact to bear fruit. Even new Chief Executives of FTSE100 firms, individuals with enormous power and huge budgets, get 'honeymoon' periods during which the City or Wall St gives them the benefit of the doubt. Projects take time to mature, structural changes such as new people, new reporting lines, new roles, etc, take time to bed down. New products need time to show whether they have a receptive market, and new processes take an age to mature and prove themselves. Cost-cutting is an expensive process in the short-term. So when I am in negotiation with a potential client firm that is looking for an interim who can meet challenging objectives for change I expect at least a six-month contract. Anything less than six months will normally result in some hard discussion about my objectives and the criteria for success, before I sign on the dotted line.

You need to take a balanced approach

The trap that a lot of interims fall into (and consultants, for that matter) is to see the client's problems as stemming from purely technical failures, and the solutions therefore as simply a matter of applying their superior know-how. As I have discussed interim management is rarely a purely technical challenge; most business problems stem from what is inside people's heads, and interims (like all managers) overlook the people issues at their peril.

This trap exists because in my experience clients often make the same mistake; they perceive their problem as a technical issue. Senior management has been told by their people that "the machine [i.e. the business process] just doesn't work". So they (the senior management) want you, the interim, to fix it. But just making the machine work is a small part of the solution, even if it is broken at all. Often it isn't; what is broken is management's relationship with the workers and consequently their (management's) understanding of the machine.

Business problems are always interconnected in a spider's web of other issues, and as an interim you need to take a holistic view, looking at products, processes, customers, suppliers and your own people. Your own superior technical knowledge is unlikely to be the silver bullet and it would be arrogant and foolish to assume that it is.

If you have read this book this far you may have detected an emerging theme; my dismay at senior management's ability to manage. My career as an industry employee and manager, as a consultant, and as an independent interim manager who has worked for many different large organisations with hugely varying cultures and approaches, has left me with a jaundiced view of management. People get to a certain level of seniority and lose touch with the shop floor, the customer and the product. For the afflicted firms the gap between senior management and the workforce is often bridged by those expensive consultants who do just what the managers should be doing; talking to the customers and front-line workers and asking them what is going wrong and what needs to be done. Of course, the consultants dress this process up to make it look like a sexy and scientific process that justifies their substantial fees: But consultancy tools such as 'workshops', 'focused interviews' and 'questionnaires' are all just blather: What the consultant is really doing is talking to the customers and workers and then telling management what they say – and that will be $3000 a day plus expenses, please... As an interim I have often found myself acting as the communications channel between senior management who no longer have a clue what really goes on, and the people on the shop floor who do understand but are never given the opportunity to say so, or whose voice is not respected. A good interim is someone who can get on with people at any level, who earns trust and respect without coming over as a smart-alec.

You need to "do detail"

Ah, the oft-heard excuse from senior managers: "I don't do detail". Of course not, sweetie. You are employed to provide your unique insight into the firm's strategic direction, your innate understanding of the marketplace, your cunning analysis of what our competitors are up to and what products we will be selling in five years' time, and your guess as to who might be interested in acquiring the firm when the share price plummets along with the profits. (And you will of course have made sure that the acquiring firm will offer you a plum role.)

Successful firms are run by managers who know how the machine works and know immediately when it is going wrong, managers who can walk the factory floor and understand exactly what each person does and who can smell a potential problem at a hundred paces. A good manager understands the figures and what they are telling him – and he knows what the figures can't tell him. A good manager does not to allow himself to be distracted by talk of potential mergers and acquisitions; he knows that the better his firm is, the stronger position he will be in when the right opportunity does come along. A good manager does detail, and so does a good interim.

How to find work as an interim

If you take nothing else away from this book this is the section that you should remember. Salesmanship is the single biggest skill that an interim needs to master if he is to make a financial success of his interim career.

In essence, the situation facing an interim manager who has the prospect of a new assignment is this:

- The client is a potential buyer. He has a problem that he wants solved, and he has a budget that may or may not be realistic. (The latter is more often the case.)

- You are a vendor. You have the skills to solve the client's problem, and you need to earn some serious money.

The challenge is that you don't necessarily know what the client's problem is (it's dangerous to assume you do) and he doesn't know what skills you have. To be realistic, the client himself probably doesn't understand the nature of his problem; he just knows he has one. (And if he thinks he understand it, he's probably wrong). And even if he does genuinely understand the problem he may not know what skills are required to solve it.

This is where your salesmanship comes in. You need to meet the client and help him gain some understanding of his problem; to arrive at a point where you at least agree where the problem lies and what the symptoms are. This involves questioning the client. The questions will depend on the nature of the client's business and the nature of his problem but are of the following type:

- When did you first become aware of the problem?

- How does the problem manifest itself?

- What solutions have you tried so far? With what results?

- What will happen if the problem isn't solved?

- What do you want me to do?

So when you are asked to attend an interview with a potential client, by all means allow him to ask questions. But remember that an interview is a dialogue; you are entitled to ask him questions. Your questions are likely to be far more to the point than his, and will no doubt prompt a more interesting and revealing discussion.

This probing process not only gives you an insight into what the problem is, it gives you an opportunity to show your understanding of it, to empathise with the client and to explain how you can help. Drawing on past experiences where you solved problems of a similar type (story-telling) can be a very powerful interview technique but be careful here; clients like to think that their problem is unique. After all, if it was simple, they would have solved it by now...

Of course, if the problem is simply that he has lost (or fired) a key member of his management team then the problem is pretty obvious and doesn't require much probing. But even in these situations I like to meet the potential client to gain an understanding of the nature of the role, and whether the previous incumbent left behind a mess or not. Why did the former incumbent leave (or get fired)? I like to know what kind of team I will be taking on; their strengths and weaknesses. There may be new challenges that the role will need to include, or the role may need to change to reflect changes in the business. Achieving this understanding helps the client paint a picture in his mind of you in the role; this is more than halfway to being offered it!

It is only when you have gained some understanding of the problem and the interim role on offer that you can move smoothly and seamlessly into explaining how your skills match the client's requirements. You do this by drawing on your past successes; the hard results you have achieved for previous clients who will be delighted to vouch for your competence. It isn't enough to say "I can do that"; you need to structure your presentation in this way:

"At Xyz firm I had a similar challenge...I solved it by... and this resulted in.... Is that the kind of result you're looking for?"

I have attended client interviews where, as a result of my questioning of the client, I have stated that I am not suitable for the role they have in mind. The client may have arrived at this conclusion himself but it is much more powerful and impressive if you take charge of that decision; there is no need for the client to send you a formal rejection letter, or for the agent (if an agent is involved) to ring you afterwards to let you know the bad news (not that they always do bother to ring, of course, but don't get me started on agents – that's for later in the book). And being the rejectee (rather than the rejected) is so much better for the ego.

Using agents

Actually I will talk about agents – you need to be warned!

21

Many recruitment agents have jumped on the bandwagon and launched interim management agencies as an adjunct to their normal recruitment operations. Some agencies claim to specialise in interim management. Some actually do specialise in interim management. It is pointless my listing them in this book because there are many of them, and they seem to come and go; they are launched with some fanfare and then quietly disappear or - if successful - get taken over by other agencies. To find out which are operating in your line of work use an internet search engine but a good place to start is the Interim Management Association; most of the reputable interim agencies are registered with the Association[3].

My experience of interim management agents is that they are a mixed bunch at best. Although there are some genuinely excellent firms out there (most of whom will be registered with the Institute of Interim Management) there is a lot of incompetence to be endured too: Let me give you my experiences of the bad ones:

- They contact me to ask whether I would be interested in a role which is wildly unsuitable for me. The poorer agents try to send as many candidates as they can find to clients, even where their suitability is not great, in the hope that this scatter-gun approach will result in one of them hitting their target. Many agents 'select' their candidates simply by conducting a word-search of the CV database, or even just a word-search of the internet. I suspect that a lot of the larger agency firms target their junior people by rewarding them for CVs sent to clients, even where the CV is not really relevant.

- The agency makes little or no attempt to find out about the role and leaves that task to their candidates, whose time they are happy to waste. What little information the agent does obtain from the client and pass on to you is turned into

---

[3] www.interimmanagement.uk.com

incomprehensible rubbish so that you end up being interviewed for a role that doesn't match the one described.

- They send two or three candidates to the client without telling you that you have competition; you are being used by the agent to give the client the impression they have a large number of candidates on their books, and you have no real prospect of getting the role. Often they put candidates forward as stalking horse; you are just there as a comparison, to make the more appropriate (or cheaper) candidate look even better.

- They offer you as an interim candidate for the same role for which they are also offering permanent candidates. As the permanent solution is inevitably the cheaper solution your time is being wasted again.

When I am contacted by an agent I don't know or trust I insist that I am told who the client is and that I am given an opportunity to meet the client to discuss the role. I am not going to waste my time (and lose a day's fee income) in attending client interviews for roles which I am not going to be offered, or would not accept even if it were offered.

I have often found myself in interesting discussions with agents about my fee rate. I talk later in this book about how to arrive at a fee rate for your services but for now you should be aware that agents usually insist when putting you forward for a role on quoting your 'standard' daily fee rate. I always point out that I don't have a 'standard' fee rate; my fees depend on the role. This is why I always try to meet the client before talking about money. If an agent is obstinate I give them a range; £1200 to £2500 per day in my case, which normally shuts the agent up and ensures that I'm not going to be bothered with time-wasting interviews.

Agents have a difficult position with regard to interim fees. On the one hand they want the fee to be as high as possible so they can take a fat margin. On the other hand they want the interim to be as cheap as possible so they win the work. You need to be very firm with agents and insist upon the fee rate you want; their margin needs to come from whatever they can persuade the client to pay over and above that. Do not let agents talk your fee rates down so that they can get a bigger margin. Have a bottom line and stick to it.

When you are discussing your fee rate with agents make it absolutely clear that the rate you are quoting is exclusive of taxes and expenses. Devious agents can put pressure on you by claiming they thought your rate was inclusive and that they have already agreed that rate with the client. Believe me, it happens, and it's a common wheeze that rookie interims fall for.

Why do client firms hire interims?

There are many reasons but here are the most common ones, all of which I have experienced:

To replace a failed predecessor

Even successful businesses make mistakes and find that they have hired or promoted a senior manager into a role which he is not competent to fill. When this realisation dawns and the firm has decided that the individual will never achieve competence (this can take time, and some organisations are more supportive - or ruthless - than others) they can start looking for ways in which to replace him with a permanent replacement.

The modern recruitment process is very protracted: The role needs to be advertised, applications sifted and interviews arranged, interviews completed (and increasingly these days there will be two or three interviews, with a formal assessment event as part of the process) and remuneration packages and start dates negotiated. After all this, most external candidates are on at least three months' notice with their current employer, and six months is by no means unusual these days. The whole process can take at least six months, and sometimes longer than that. So in the absence of an immediately available internal candidate an interim is the most obvious solution.

Taking over from a failed predecessor is difficult in some ways, and easy in others. The difficulties come from inheriting an often demoralised team that requires a change in direction. Believe me, changing a team's attitudes and approach is hard work. Often the team's relationship with its customers has broken down and this will require retrieval; again, no picnic. Generally, when one takes over from a failed predecessor the challenge is to identify the changes required and to implement them; this takes energy and determination, good analytical skills, and leadership.

I actually look forward to these situations because anything I do differently from my predecessor has a chance of getting results, and even small successes make me look good. As an interim, if you have confidence in your abilities, inheriting a mess is something to be relished.

To replace a successful predecessor

In some ways this is a harder situation for an interim to inherit than the above. A successful predecessor who has retired, gone on sabbatical or maternity/paternity leave or just left for pastures new is a hard act to follow; the challenge is in keeping intact what she or he left behind and perhaps at best looking for small additional improvements. It is normally a mistake in such situations for an interim to seek to make drastic changes; an interim is better advised to keep the ship on the same course and hand over to the eventual permanent successor pretty much the happy situation that you inherited. No-one is going to thank you for throwing everything up in the air and leaving your successor to pick up the pieces; you will only be criticised for trying to fix something that wasn't broken.

I must admit that I find these situations rather disappointing. Acting as a kind of night-watchman and simply keeping things steady until the permanent replacement arrives is not my idea of fun. I, like most people, want to make a difference. It is also more difficult to demand a high fee rate in such situations; clients don't feel like paying much to a night-watchman. Crisis assignments are more lucrative, more interesting, and (if you manage them successfully) more satisfying.

They are of course more stressful, too, and perhaps the ideal life as an interim is one of a mixed diet of assignments.

To head up a new project or department

Firms sometimes find that they are planning a project or development which they don't have sufficient or appropriate internal resource to manage. This is often the case when the firm is exploring new business opportunities in areas where it has had little or no previous exposure. An interim can be the ideal solution in such a situation.

To act as the hatchet man

Not infrequently an interim is tasked with the unpleasant job of swinging the axe within a department; identifying candidates for redundancy and managing them out of the business. Interims are ideal for this because:

a) Interims are unlikely to have personal attachments to anyone in the department and can therefore take a more dispassionate and objective approach to selecting the unlucky candidates;

b) The interim is not going to be around in the long-term to act as the focus of the survivors' mistrust and disgruntlement;

c) It isn't easy recruiting a permanent person to join a firm which is undergoing a period of 'downsizing'.

Making someone redundant is a thoroughly unpleasant task, probably one of the worst things a manager can be asked to do in the course of a career. Sacking someone for misconduct or incompetence is much, much easier than identifying a blameless individual and telling him that he no longer has a job. If you find yourself in the role of hatchet man (or woman) there are some key things to get right:

Be very careful to apply objective, measurable criteria in selecting the unlucky candidates. The client firm's HR department will normally be fully involved in determining what criteria and process should be applied, and you should stick to the agreed prescription.

Having said all of this, my tendency when acting as a hatchet man is to see the senior people within my department as the most likely candidates for redundancy on the grounds that:

a) They have the bigger salaries and therefore represent the easiest way of making the cost savings required. This can depend of course on their redundancy benefits, and I have experienced some very strange accounting approaches in such situations in which my client firm seems only to focus on annual salary budget cuts and ignores the actual - and sometimes huge - cost of paying someone to go.

b) They are in my experience often the less useful members of the department. I have a perhaps unreasonable bias towards junior staff who are often the unsung and under-rewarded performers.

c) Getting rid of the top layer of management within a department or organisation allows me more direct access to the people who do the work; the 'engine room', thereby making my job - of changing the way the department or organisation works - easier.

d) The senior people, I have found, are more likely to be the ones who resent my being there and who do their best to divert my efforts towards positive change.

e) Losing the senior people allows me some room to promote the unsung heroes, or at least extend their roles and give them a chance to show what they can do, with often surprising results.

What counts as success for interims?

Being an Interim Internal Audit, Risk or Compliance Director (or any combination of these) to a large and complicated organisation is hardly a vocation. It is often boring, usually frustrating, and sometimes scary, particularly when I am caught between a complacent and often inept board of directors and a bloodthirsty, all-powerful and usually incompetent regulator. To put it bluntly I am only in this game for the money, so success for me is measured in financial terms. My leaving the Big Four consultancy environment was simply a way of doing the same work for the same clients but ensuring that the money I earned arrived in my bank account and not that of my boss who, it seemed to me, was more than rich enough already.

Yes, there is some satisfaction to be gained from a job well done, and I am very grateful for the plaudits I have received from happy clients; particularly because a good reference helps me get the next piece of work and keeps my daily fee rate high. I also treasure the thanks I have received from past colleagues, and if I have been able to help them in their careers (something I try hard to do) I genuinely get a kick out of that.

Another motivation for leaving full-time employment was the opportunity to gain the 'work/life balance' that my former employers kept promising but which I never seemed to achieve. As a self-employed interim I take far more holiday than I could as an employee. Last summer ago for example I set aside the whole of July and August as holiday, which was just wonderful. There are few employment contracts that permit that kind of freedom.

A big plus to life as a self-employed consultant and interim is that I am free to give the advice that I think is right for the client, and not the advice that my consultancy employers would like me to give. The well-known consultancy firms seem to prefer client 'solutions' (everything is a solution these days) that involve lots of junior consultants engaged for lengthy periods to conduct detailed and interminable analyses. The more complex the analysis and solution the better, particularly if it involves the consultancy firm having to do more work. (For a glimpse of my approach to clients' problems see Andrew Gordon's Code of Ethics.)

Finally, being a self-employed interim has allowed me to simplify my life. I am no longer responsible for hordes of junior consultants who need to be sold out to clients even though they know 1% of the square root of diddly-squat about the business that has engaged them. I am not responsible for their supervision or training and I don't have to give, or receive, appraisals. I don't have to fill out grossly complicated timesheets designed so that my boss, who doesn't understand what I do or the advice I give, can somehow claim to be 'managing' me even though he never turns up at a client site to see me in action and doesn't read the reports I write. (If he did he wouldn't understand them.) Nor do I have to negotiate through tortuous expense claim and billing processes; my wonderful Company Secretary Vicky deals with all of that, and it takes her no time at all.

So, a successful year for me is one where I earn the most money for the least effort, and have as much fun as possible in doing so. Isn't that everyone's idea of business success? Happy clients are important, too, but I'm not sure whether their satisfaction is important to me for its own sake or because I need to keep them happy so that they are prepared to pay my high fee rate and recommend me to another client who is willing to pay an even higher fee rate.

The assignment contract – the legal requirements

These will vary according to the assignment, the organisation and the role of the interim manager but it will normally include:

- A high-level description of the project
- The planned timescale for the assignment
- Any arrangements for extending the assignment, if appropriate
- Critical success factors – the results looked for
- The fee structure, including payment terms, expenses, etc
- Confidentiality requirements

In my experience the client's legal or HR department will provide a draft contract, which I always read carefully. So must you. They are often adaptions of the firm's template employment contract and the adaptions can be naïve, and sometimes nonsense. I am not at all shy about suggesting sensible re-drafts. Agency contracts (where an agency is involved) can be better written but should still be read with care.

Conducting staff appraisals when you're an interim

As an interim you will normally be asked to take on the management responsibilities of the person whose role you are occupying, including that person's appraisal duties. This is one of the main ways in which interims differ from consultants.

Appraisals are something I have strong views about. I have been the victim and perpetrator of many, and to those I have appraised, let me say now that I am terribly, terribly sorry. To those who have appraised me, let me say that you were all wide of the mark and that I haven't changed my behaviour one bit. (If I have, it's not as a result of your appraisal.) I *like* being Andrew Gordon, and most of my clients seem to like me, too.

Appraisals are energy-sapping and demoralising experiences for all concerned. I can't understand why feedback should be a formalised annual event where behaviour long past and forgotten is dredged up, and where 'key performance indicators' that are irrelevant and easy to manipulate are discussed in all seriousness. A good manager (and to be fair I have known a few) will demonstrate to me his own competence and watch me try to emulate. When I get it wrong, I know I've got it wrong; or he will tell me straight away and not wait until an annual appraisal to ask "how was it for you?".

Formal appraisal processes (sorry, I've started now so I'm going to finish) are based on a myth; that there is such a thing as objectivity. There is not. How can there be? – there is no absolute truth; observations made by any human being are just that; observations, about something that happened in the past, weakened by memory, flavoured by perception, cultural influences and emotions, expressed in language that is inevitably a limited medium in which to express thought and which is prone to ambiguity. When the observations are about another human being's behaviours and attitudes you can be sure that objectivity is impossible, no matter how hard both parties try.

When asked to conduct appraisals during an interim assignment I have of course met client needs in this direction but I am very, very careful to be as fair and as open-minded as I can be, and to explain that my observations are simply a poor attempt on my part to explain how I perceive the other person to be. And I try to restrain discussion to that which can be measured empirically; a salesman's performance (for example) can to some extent be measured in figures (number of appointments made with potential clients, number of presentations given, value of sales achieved, etc). I am very wary about discussion aimed at identifying what behaviours should be employed to improve these figures; my cowardly inclination is to allow the appraisee (horrible word I know) to draw his own conclusions about the appropriate action to take.

In seeking a client's feedback on my own performance I prefer to set up weekly meetings to discuss what has happened in the past week, and what I propose to do for the next week. Friday mornings are ideal, when everything is fresh in my and my client's mind and the weekend will give me time to digest the feedback and prepare for a fresh assault. By having these meetings weekly I ensure that if I am going astray I have not had time to go too far wrong and the damage is repairable. I have no formal agenda for these 'one-to-ones'; I tend to prepare for them by simply writing a list of things I want to discuss with my client as I go through the week (assuming such items are not urgent).

Your first few days

Getting off to a good start

So you've won your first assignment. Well done! This is the most important assignment you will ever undertake in your interim career, because if it is successful it will be the launch pad to a new working life, and probably a new life outside work, too. Becoming a professional interim allows, even forces, a fundamental change in how work fits into the rest of your life. However, if your first assignment fails it is going to be very difficult for you to find a next assignment, and very difficult for you to approach that assignment with the courage and enthusiasm you need to make it a success. Your behaviour and performance during the first week or two is crucial. Getting off to a good start on an assignment is absolutely vital; a bad start is very hard to put right.

Hopefully you will have done your research before you arrive. You will have a good idea of the organisation's structure, its remit, products, services, markets, etc. You will have some understanding of its strengths and weaknesses, its opportunities and threats (the old SWOT analysis). The internet has made this kind of research ludicrously easy, and I am often surprised just how much information organisations make available online, sometimes quite sensitive information. You will of course if possible have used your network to get the inside track on the important stuff; who really who drives the organisation, the political agendas, where the money is coming from, and where its going, etc. You will have taken from the agency - where one is involved - any information they have available. (And taken it with a pinch of salt.)

When you turn up on Day One don't expect the organisation to have made preparations for your arrival, or for key staff to even be aware that you are arriving. But if you are lucky the organisation will have done some things in readiness:

- Set you up on the organisation's intranet and given you an email ID, with access to the records you will need;
- Provided you with a works computer;
- Informed people of your arrival and the role you will be taking;
- Allocated a desk, PA, parking space and anything else you might need.

In my experience these preparations are not always made so I like to check with the client before my arrival to ensure that they are in hand. It is also a good idea before arriving to arrange for a tour of the building on Day One, and some introductory sessions with a few key individuals. The last thing you want is to arrive and find that the things and people you need to see are not available.

Why you should not "hit the ground running"

"We need someone who can hit the ground running." How often have I heard this said by prospective clients when looking for an interim? It is of course complete tosh; one only needs to explore the analogy to see how daft it is:

> *The Paratrooper Commander lands in a crumpled heap behind enemy lines. Picking himself up he quickly unbuckles his parachute and looks around him. As he was the first to jump, he is the first to land. Hitching his kit higher up his back he starts to sprint for the horizon; he isn't sure if he's running in the right direction. One by one his men are hitting the ground around him. He ignores them, and carries on running...*

Stupid, isn't it? What the Commander would of course do is this: He would wait for his men to land, and gather them together. He would perform a quick headcount to make sure everyone had landed safely, complete with their vital kit. He would look at the map to ensure that he knew the location in which they had landed, and check the compass to make sure of his objective's heading. The plan quickly confirmed he would give the word to his men, and move them out...

The Paratrooper Commander might only take a few minutes to do this. You should expect it to take a few days and more likely a few weeks, during which you will check your resources, take in the lie of the land, formulate a plan, and brief your team. During that process you should *not* be running anywhere; you should be listening, and questioning, and listening, and questioning.

The first few days

The first few days of an interim assignment are exciting but they can be stressful, and you must expect to feel uncomfortable at the very least. You are entering an organisation about which you know only what you have been told, or which is publicly available. You are meeting people you don't know and trying desperately to remember their names and what they do. You may even find yourself attending meetings and being asked questions which you can't answer (if you tried you would probably make a fool of yourself). People's expectations of you will be high and you will feel under pressure to impress them with your knowledge and experience.

Try to relax. Remind yourself that the anxiety you are feeling is normal and to be expected. Don't try to impress; you will have plenty of time to make your mark during the length of the assignment. If you are asked any difficult questions simply say that you need time to understand and that you'll get back to the questioner with an answer. Or even better, suggest that you meet the questioner to discuss the issue in a more relaxed context.

Be deprecating about yourself; no-one likes a smart-alec. Use humour only when you are confident that your brand of humour works; off-colour jokes or awkward attempts at a wise-crack are just embarrassing for you and your listeners.

Take deep breaths, and remember to smile.

Handover periods – how to use them

You may have an opportunity to meet your predecessor before he leaves the organisation. This is not at all unusual and you should take full advantage of it. Pump the guy (or lady) dry of information. Be nice to him; he will be wary of you, and may be disaffected with his employer. You need to get on the right side of him, so be tactful, cautious and friendly; he needs to trust you and know that you are not going to go back to the boss and tell him what an idiot you think he is. Avoid any discussion about the reason he is leaving, if it is at all sensitive. You are just there to get the facts and understand the issues. But in my experience even disaffected predecessors have been very helpful; there is after all such a thing as professionalism, and most people try their best to show how well they were doing their job.

Avoid giving any opinion about how well or badly your predecessor was doing his job. I know this may seem obvious but it is just as well to make sure. People are understandably very sensitive about their job and their performance, even when their departure is for the right reasons, and they are not going to welcome you telling them what they have been doing wrong all these years. You should also remember that your first impressions are almost certainly going to be wide of the mark; you need to properly understand the pressures and difficulties your predecessor faced before arriving at any judgements. As one professional to another I am always happy to offer my congratulations to my predecessor where I genuinely believe he has done an excellent job, without being patronising about it. I am also happy to say just how wonderful a job I think he's done, even when I am quietly realising that the guy's an idiot. What harm can it do?

During the handover period with your predecessor you should be making discreet notes for discussion with your client boss later on; you need to find out what your predecessor did that your boss liked and didn't like. Just because your predecessor did things in a certain way doesn't mean you have to follow suit. As an interim you have the opportunity to reinvent the role if you think that is appropriate but bear in mind Andrew Gordon's Code of Ethics rule number 1 (If It Isn't Broken Don't Fix It) and also check with your client boss first to see how amenable he is to the changes you have in mind. Do this cautiously. Avoid appearing to criticise your predecessor; test the water by asking innocuous questions that seek to elicit your boss' view of the service he has received to date.

During the handover period you should focus on getting the hard facts; what your predecessor does, his daily activities, the meetings he attends and the information he uses. You don't want to start your assignment by dropping a ball in the first few days. It is also a good idea to obtain the soft facts; his views on what the big issues and challenges are, his understanding of the political landscape. You don't have to accept his view of it as correct or realistic, of course, but even the wrong view is useful to know and potentially revealing; it will help you avoid making the same mistakes.

Finally, bear in mind that any impression you give your predecessor will get back to your boss, your peers and your subordinates. So if you come across as a know-all don't expect their co-operation.

Pitfalls for the unwary - how to avoid them

Be wary of the early requests for support

Some years ago I acted as a Compliance Project Manager for a consumer credit organisation that was in some difficulty. Two days into my new role the Operations Director introduced himself and after a genial chat over coffee he invited me to "look over" a presentation containing his recommendations for the firm's future sales and collections strategy. I was flattered that he would seek my opinion, and happy to read his slides. The presentation seemed to me perfectly sensible and offered no major challenges from my viewpoint, and I responded with an email saying just that. What the Operations Director didn't tell me was that the presentation was going to be made to the Board the next day – with comments to the effect that the presentation had the "approval" of the new Compliance Project Manager. His presentation bombed and he left the organisation "by mutual agreement" a few days later.

I learned afterwards that the Operations Director had been fighting for his political life and that his presentation to the Board was his last ditch attempt at keeping his job. Everyone (except me) knew that he was due for the chop, and that his recommendations were completely contrary to the views of several key players on the Board. Needless to say, it soon became common knowledge that I had given my "approval" of his presentation, and so my reputation was sullied; I had unknowingly jumped a political divide within the firm, and landed on the wrong side. (And in political debates the wrong side is always the side that loses.)

Don't make the same mistake. If, within the first few days or weeks of your assignment you are asked for your opinion on a key issue, give it warily. Ask how the opinion is going to be used, and in what context. Better still, try to avoid giving it at all.

Don't jump to conclusions

"The issue seems to be that our key products are too expensive. We are spending too much on development - we need to reduce our cost base and get our pricing down, and concentrate on selling what we make today".

You've opened your big mouth in a meeting and instantly made an enemy of that half of the business that is convinced that what is required is investment in new product development, supported by price hikes across the existing product range.

This is why you need to take your time in arriving at an analysis of what has gone wrong and why. You need to gather your facts, get everyone's opinion, and gain an insight into the political landscape. Test your ideas out in a low-risk environment; check them with your boss in a quiet one-to-one discussion before giving everyone the benefit of your worldly wisdom.

Make sure you're solving the right problem

Client do sometimes give interims very specific objectives to be achieved during your assignment period but my general experience is that I am given rather vague directions along the lines of "we need you to sort the department out", or " the project needs a new focus", or "just make it happen".

Your first few weeks on an assignment is your opportunity to arrive at your own conclusions about what the problem is and how it can best be solved. If, that is, there is a problem at all; sometimes there isn't and all that is required is a steady hand on the tiller. Once you've come to a reasoned conclusion, hopefully based on fact and observation rather than gut instinct and assumption, discuss with your client boss your views and see whether a more sensible and defined set of objectives can be settled upon. It is the objectives you agree now that will define whether you succeed or not and whether you get a good reference or not, and references are the lifeblood of the interim manager. Obviously, make sure the objectives are achievable, and ideally that achievement of them can be demonstrated in some empirical way; you want no argument from your client at the end of the project that you "missed your target".

Failure to take this vital step during the first few weeks of an assignment could result in you trying to solve problems that don't exist, or are inconsequential, or are impossible to solve with the time and resources at your command, or that the client wasn't really all that bothered about.

Don't bite off more than you can chew

An interim manager builds his reputation - and his fee rate - by developing a track record of hard, demonstrable results. Your success as an interim is based on your ability to achieve what needs to be, and can be, achieved. A CV which states that you nearly solved x, or almost achieved y, or that you implemented z but the CV doesn't (because it can't) show what an important contribution it made to the firm's well-being, is not the kind of CV that is going to win you the next lucrative assignment. So you need to ensure that at each assignment you set out to achieve the achievable and the important. You need to agree with your client objectives based on the time you have, the resources available, and your client firm's willingness, readiness and level of enthusiasm for what you have in mind. If your CV shows that you spent six months trying to push a boulder uphill, only to see it roll back down when you left, your interim career is going to be less than successful.

How to introduce yourself to the team

Try to put yourself in the shoes of your client and your colleagues. They probably know very little about you, and they may even be scared of you. They might have doubts about your ability to take on their department or project. As you will be playing a significant part in their working day, and potentially in their careers, they want to know more about you. There are some key steps you should take to ensure a smooth introduction to the business:

Assuming you have taken over responsibility for a team that is more than, say, six people, it is often a good idea to get everyone in a room and give them a brief discussion on who you are, what your objectives are, and what your intended approach will be. For a team of fewer than six people a less formal introduction would normally be appropriate; a chat over coffee would be less stiff.

Keep it generic at this stage - after all you might change your mind later - but give your team some sense of what you stand for; your philosophy, what you feel strongly about, what you can't stand, and where you see things going in your field. Try to do it off the cuff, without (and this is important) using Powerpoint slides or flipcharts. Use humour, share some experiences from your career, invite questions, and show them you are interested in them as people and determined to help them succeed.

Some interims like to distribute their CV to their new client team. I am always reluctant to do this, because a) although my CV is good there is always someone in the organisation it will fail to impress ("Hey – this guy's not even an MBA! – and he got his degree from *where?*") and b) even if my CV is impressive it might have an impact I am not looking for. CVs by their nature tend to be boastful. I prefer telling people what I've done in the past as part of my oral introduction to the team, or when I meet people one-to-one. The air of mystery that surrounds a high-level interim when he arrives at a new client firm is no bad thing and I don't want it to evaporate too quickly.

How to introduce yourself to individuals within the team

As well as getting your team together as a team and introducing who you are and giving them an idea of what you stand for, you need to meet each individual team member and establish a relationship. At the start of a new assignment I take the time to meet all my reports (including, most importantly, the most junior) for from ten minutes to an hour. Let me tell you why this is important and why you must do it too:

Most business problems are far from new and intractable. Someone, somewhere will understand the problem, and someone, somewhere, will have the solution. The person who understands the problem and the person who has the solution may not be one and the same, and they may never talk to each other. Neither may even realise there is a problem, or that they have the solution. So, your job as an interim is to talk to them and to bring your worldly experience and insight to bear; to identify the people who might have the answers. This means talking to everyone but particularly (and I cannot emphasise this enough) the junior staff, because they are the ones who are closest to the customer, who deal with the issues every day and who find ways around the problem you are trying to solve.

My experience of interviewing senior colleagues is that they are too keen on trying to prove how good they are, and telling you what they think you want to hear, to be of interest. Yes, yes, you need to interview them too, but *later*. I like to talk to the juniors first. If nothing else it is great fun to watch the blind panic as the seniors realise that their direct reports are being given an opportunity to get a few things off their chest!

And of course you also need to talk to everyone outside your department who might have some useful insights, or who will be a supplier to, or customer of, your department or project, or even just an observer. A good idea is to use your arrival at the business and your lack of knowledge of it as an excuse to also talk to people outside the firm; its suppliers, customers and even its competitors, if you can persuade them to let you in. If nothing else you will be gaining potential valuable business contacts, and you never know; you may stumble upon something very interesting indeed. In my line of work as a risk management interim to the financial services industry I also make a point of arranging an early "introductory" meeting with the client firm's auditors and other external authorities; the regulators, for example. If nothing else it helps to know who you are going to be dealing with. Being on first-name terms with people is an important step to a successful relationship.

This is the process that management consultants normally follow when conducting their 'fact find' of the client business. I won't bang on again about why firms pay expensive management consultants to ask their own staff what is wrong and what they should do about it but you as an interim should learn this simple technique. It will pay dividends, believe me. Your diary will fill up quickly, so do this as soon as you can, while it is still relatively empty.

Don't make the mistake of trying to impress at these early meetings. You are there to learn, not to display your own talents. Ask intelligent questions, then shut up and listen. Let them do the talking.

You should also avoid the mistake I once made of not making it clear why I wanted to interview everyone in a 50-strong department I had inherited from a failed predecessor. A rumour quickly developed that my interviews were a clandestine attempt to identify candidates for redundancy. Until I cottoned onto this the interviews were bizarre and unhelpful; I found myself on the receiving end of carefully rehearsed presentations, including full-colour slides and CVs. Make it clear to everyone why you want to talk to them, and impress upon them that what they say will be kept confidential. You want their honest opinion of life in the department and the organisation, not evidence of their employability. Emphasise that you do not want them to prepare anything at all.

Some potential questions to ask (in no particular order, and you don't need to ask them all):

41

1. Give me a brief resume of your career.

2. What is your role?

3. What are we trying to achieve?

4. What are you trying to achieve?

5. What do you like about working here?

6. What don't you like about working here?

7. How do we measure how good we are?

8. In what areas should we improve?

9. What would you change if you could?

10. Are you happy working here?

11. Where do you see your career going?

12. What is stopping you from achieving your personal goals?

I could go on but you get the idea. The trick is to ask open, unthreatening questions that invite a discussion. Don't forget to thank them for their honesty and ideas, and to assure them that what they have said is confidential. Invite them to come and talk to you at any time.

Do make the effort to attend lunches, after-work drinks sessions and other social events. People are often more inclined to speak freely in such situations, particularly after they have had a drink or two, and you often get the real gossip rather than the party line. But don't be seen to be trying to get them drunk, and don't get drunk yourself; in that direction lies career suicide.

Do these things, and believe me, nine times out of ten the answers to many of your client's problems will be presented to you on a plate within the first few weeks of your new assignment. Your skill is to recognise the problems and answers for what they are, and to make the answers happen – but your client will be deeply impressed with your insight.

How to make an assignment work

Record your observations and successes

For each new assignment I buy a new hardback A4 notebook which I keep with me at all times. In this notebook I record anything of interest; any interesting fact, a quotable statement from someone I've been talking to, names and contact details of key staff members, notes of interviews or meetings, scribbles of draft presentations I intend to make. I also glue or staple other documents into it that are of long-term interest; key emails or letters, address and telephone lists, company structure charts, product lists, price lists, maps showing the firm's distribution geography, etc, etc. My notebook quickly becomes a scrapbook full of snippets of information and it is amazing just how often the information I have stored away is of use when I'm in a tight spot.

This notebook is also fantastically valuable when you leave an organisation at the end of an assignment. Believe me it is very difficult to remember anything about a past assignment once you have embarked on another, and if the assignment was two or three jobs back it will all be a blank. Your notebook will come in very handy for reminding you of people's names, job titles, the work you did, your achievements, etc.

I also use my notebook to record my private (at this stage) observations about the client situation I have been asked to manage. I then use these observations as the basis of my regular (weekly!) one-to-one discussions with my client boss in which I share my thoughts about the challenges facing me, and what needs to be done and how.

43

I avoid turning these observations into a formal presentation. An informal one-to-one with your client boss discussion gives you the opportunity to feel what impact your comments are having on your listener; if he bristles then you know you have touched a raw nerve and that you need to back off or soft-pedal. You are looking for a dialogue, not a monologue. The aim is simple; to ensure that you and your client boss have the same issues and priorities. If you don't do this you can easily find yourself barking up the wrong tree and solving the wrong problems.

You should also make a note of any small successes and good results you can legitimately claim as your own. By the end of the assignment you will have a list of triumphs which you would not have been able to remember if you had left it until then, and you can use the list to remind the client of just how good you were, before they give you that glowing reference. The big successes should of course be transferred to your CV!

Fitting in

All organisations have a culture. As an interim life is going to be much easier if you make the effort to fit into that culture as soon as you can. This means being cautious when challenging established shibboleths and the received wisdom that exists in any organisation. By all means question a firm's objectives and approach but be careful when doing so; there is a fine line between being seen as a breath of fresh air or being seen as rocking the boat. Formal meetings are not the time and place to ask difficult questions. It is better to tentatively test your ideas out in informal one-to-one conversations where your questions and comments are not going to be embarrass, expose or threaten. Do this by asking gently probing questions such as "have we ever tried…" or "what was the background to that decision?"

If you really do feel that the status quo ante is not an option (and change is essential to the long-term survival of most organisations) then you need to remember the two golden rules for making change happen:

44

1) It is very difficult to *persuade* anyone to do anything. Permanent and meaningful changes in behaviour only occur when a change in attitude has already occurred; people do what they believe to be right, not what they are told to do. Belief and desire are much more powerful and more long-lasting motivators than reward and fear.

2) The best way to achieve attitudinal change is to help someone discover for themselves that their existing viewpoint is not sustainable. You do this by asking questions, the answers to which lead people to a different perspective. In this way no-one feels that they have been 'persuaded' to move; they have made the journey for themselves.

Remember that you can never, ever, win an argument: Even if you 'prove' your viewpoint by force of logic you will almost certainly have damaged a relationship in the process.

This process is even more important when one is an outsider and new to the organisation. People do not readily accept the viewpoint of a Johnny-come-lately. Interims should remember this.

Don't rubbish your predecessor

I have said it before but it is worth repeating. This is a golden rule for interim managers. No matter how appalling the mess you have inherited it is absolutely unacceptable and unprofessional for you to pour scorn on your predecessor. You don't know what pressures he was under, or what obstacles were put in his way. Remember the old American proverb: "Never criticise a man until you have walked a mile in his moccasins." (Don't worry, that's as cheesy as this book gets.) If you think your predecessor was wrong or incompetent the best way to demonstrate that is by quietly doing better, not by telling the world how and why he was wrong. Perhaps at the end of the assignment, when you have solved the problems your predecessor left behind, you will be entitled to some quiet personal satisfaction - but not until then, and even at that point your satisfaction should be restrained to some hard facts contained within your CV. Bad-mouthing your predecessor isn't going to win you friends, enhance your professional image, improve your reputation or increase your marketability.

Also remember that the person who hears your criticism may have liked and admired the person whose performance you are denigrating, and may be saying to himself: "Okay smart-alec, let's see you do better". And do not be so naïve as to assume that your criticism will not get back to the individual concerned; it will.

My general experience as an interim is that I start an assignment surprised at how bad my predecessor has left things, and finish the assignment understanding why. It can take six months to walk that mile.

Managing your team

Clearly a good interim manager needs good management skills. But as I said in the introduction this is not a book about management; it's a book about interim management. I am not going to lecture you on how to manage because you probably already have management skills which are at least as good as mine. There are however some management issues relating to life as an interim which you may want to think about:

Don't get swallowed up by the task.

Interims are often introduced to situations where the task in hand - the problem or set of problems, the project, the technical challenges, etc - has reached a critical and urgent stage. Solving the problem is the immediate objective. It is easy in such situations to focus on that task, and to lose sight of the people who are helping you achieve the task. You need to bear in mind that your team, peers and seniors need to understand the problem, they need to be taught how to solve it for themselves, and they need encouragement and confidence to try to do so. They need to understand what you are trying to achieve and how, why they have failed in the past, and what needs to be done to ensure that they succeed in the future.

You should not forget that your own performance will depend upon the performance of your team. If your team is feeling bruised, demoralised and neglected you are not going to achieve your objectives by perpetuating that state of affairs. You have to rebuild their confidence and energy levels. This means you need to focus on them as people; you need to understand what motivates them, what is getting in the way of their own personal success, what their own goals are, and how best to achieve a change in their behaviour.

Just getting the result is not enough; you need to help the organisation achieve the result. As an interim you are not just a trouble-shooter. 'Red' Adair - an extreme example of an interim manager - put out oil and gas well fires but he also taught other people how to put out fires. And how to prevent them.

Learn to be humble

Do not assume that because a particular problem has developed within an organisation it's because no one else in the organisation (other than you, naturally) understands the problem and has the skills to manage it. It may well be the case that other people in the organisation understand the problem and have the skills to solve it but have never been given the opportunity to demonstrate this. Perhaps they are too junior to be heard, or have never been asked for their opinion. One of your objectives as an interim is to find these people and to bring them forward as future managers of some or all of the challenges you have been given. Who knows, they may even be able to take over from you entirely. Without exception I have found that all of the large firms that have engaged me as an interim already employ people who have a very good idea of what the problems are and what needs to be done about them. These people are often quite junior, which is why they have not been heard up to now. One of the more enjoyable aspects of my life as an interim has been bringing these people into the sunlight and watching them grow.

Telling people that they need to "do better" is not going to help

An interim will often be asked to take over the running of an under-performing team. Their morale may be at rock-bottom, they may be the pariah of the organisation, and to cap it all their old boss has left and this new smart-alec interim manager has come in and started telling them where they've been going wrong...

Many other people have said it much better than I can. Here's one:

> *"At any moment each person is always doing the very best he can, based on his total conscious and non-conscious prevailing awareness and which is within his capabilities, energy, time, and developed talents and abilities. If people are always doing the very best they can, it is illogical and irrational to expect them to do better. What is the reason this concept is so important to understand? If it is true, then it is counterproductive to criticize someone for not meeting or conforming to an expectation or standard until they have the awareness of the benefits they will receive by conforming. What needs to exist is for people to be made aware of how they will get better results, by pointing out the consequences of their behavior and giving them the choice and opportunity to make adjustments."*
> (Sidney Madwed, American speaker, author, consultant, poet.)

Conscious incompetence is a rare thing in working life. Few people know they are incompetent; if they did, they would either take the necessary action to become competent, or find a job for which they are already competent. Research consistently shows that where conscious incompetence does exist it causes significant stress for the individual, stress which normally causes the sufferer to seek alternative employment. It follows that most incompetent people are *unconsciously* competent; they really, genuinely do not know that they are incompetent, so just telling them to "do better" is not going to achieve anything. *Showing* people precisely how and where their performance falls short of acceptability, and how to do better, is the way to make change happen. Help in recognising the need for improvement, and help in achieving that improvement, coupled with praise and, wherever appropriate and possible, reward, is a hugely more powerful way achieving performance improvement than negative criticism.

Dress appropriately

As an interim you should normally choose to dress to the level of your immediate colleagues. If they turn up in jeans and tee-shirt then being the only suit in the office is not going to be conducive to being seen as "one of us". Having said this, if in doubt it is much better to dress up rather than dress down; at worst a suit will simply mark you out as a man or woman of authority, a professional consultant. This can work if you don't particularly need to be seen as "one of us".

Men should avoid jewellery and chunky multi-function watches the size of ashtrays. A wedding ring is of course perfectly acceptable. Visible tattoos used to be absolutely verboten in most office-based work environments and cultures, although this attitude probably marks me out as a man of yesterday's generation; even professional people these days seem to try and prove their 'individuality' by following the common herd and inking themselves. I don't think this is a good thing for a professional person but that's just my view.

Women seem able to wear whatever they like to an office these days but my advice to female interims is the same: If in doubt, dress smartly and keep the bare flesh to a minimum. Cleavage is never a good idea.

The image you are looking for is one of quiet professionalism so any flashiness, ostentation or obvious slavery to fashion should be avoided. Anything that draws attention to the way you dress should be avoided.

Understanding the politics

To state the obvious, an organisation is made up of people. People are irrational, even when they think they are being rational; they have emotional needs and problems, strengths and weaknesses, and hates and desires. There is no such thing as an apolitical organisation; I am sure that even a silent order of monks will have its doctrinal schisms.

One of the reasons that some people explain their attraction to an interim management career is because they see it as a way of avoiding the 'office politics' they hated as a permanent employee. They fondly imagine that as an interim one can rise above the fray. After all, as an interim you are there to do a job, achieve results and get out, without having to engage in all of the jockeying for position, the toadying and sniping.

The people who think that interim management offers these advantages could not be more wrong.

As an interim you need to possess finely tuned political antennae. If you don't gain an early understanding of the political landscape within a client organisation you are likely to make some terrible and embarrassing mistakes which will prove very difficult to undo, and you will be easy meat for the clever political operators that exist in every organisation. You need to know which way the wind is blowing, who's in and who's out, who the winners and losers are going to be. The trick is not necessarily to *engage* in the politics but to understand them and to avoid blundering into them and making a fool of yourself. As an interim new to a client assignment you will be seen as an independent with some immunity from the pressure to take sides. You need to be aware of what the sides are so that you don't allow yourself to be dragged unwittingly from your neutral position into the thick of battle.

I know the language I have used in the above paragraph is less than specific but that is what office politics is like, isn't it? - something that is felt rather than necessarily clearly stated. Just take care out there, that's all.

How to manage your client boss

As an interim you will end up working for all sorts of people as clients (your temporary bosses). The relationship you have with this person will not, and should not, be the same as the kind of relationship with bosses you will have had as a permanent employee. The differences are small but important:

- As an interim you will have a much shorter timescale in which to impress your client boss. Permanent employees are used to annual cycles in which objectives are agreed and then achievement of them reviewed during an annual appraisal. (I know that it shouldn't happen like that but in reality it nearly always does.) Interim assignments *can* last a year, if not longer, but are normally measured in months. So you have a much shorter time in which to agree objectives and to demonstrate your achievement of them. This places much greater emphasis on regular meetings with your client boss to make that demonstration. I try to get agreement to weekly meetings with my client, in which I will take more care to get recognition of my progress than a permanent employee would bother to do. (Perhaps permanent employees should take a leaf out of this book? – if they did they might find that that promotion is more within reach.)

- Employers of any quality will normally take some responsibility for their employees' career development. It is obviously in their interests to do so. But an interim's client doesn't give a tinker's cuss about the interim's career; he just wants his problem solved and the interim out of there, pronto. Conversations between an interim and his temporary boss tend therefore to be focused on the task in hand, with no horizon beyond that.

- Employees expect and deserve respect from their managers. As an interim you need to be realistic; you are a temporary contractor, Sunshine, and if you don't like it you know what you can do. So if you find that your temporary boss is an irredeemable piece of ordure you just need to grit your teeth and get on with solving the problem, so that you can get out of there and onto the next assignment as soon as possible. Don't go bleating to HR or whoever about what a swine he is to work for; they are not going to be interested.

If you are considering an interim career don't be too disheartened by this. True, I've had temporary bosses who were incompetent, or devious, or bullying, and even crooked, and I have also worked for people for whom I have had great respect. I've learned from both experiences. That is one of the great advantages of the interim life; you cram a lot of experience into a short time, and thereby gain a much wider perspective than a permanent employee buried in a large organisation. And if you do find yourself working for an ogre you can always console yourself with the knowledge that you will be out of there before long.

Whatever type of boss you find yourself working for, you need to manage him. I have already talked about how to make sure that you give him what he wants (and how to ensure that he recognises that he is getting what he wants) but you need to go further than that: You need to put yourself in your temporary boss's shoes and try to understand what he really wants - and this means more than just a solution to his stated problem.

He needs to feel good. And I mean *really* good. He needs to feel that by hiring you he has found someone who will hide his mistakes and weaknesses and help him achieve what he needs to gain kudos. He needs to know that you will make him look good in the eyes of his boss, and that you are not going to expose him. He needs help to forget that he has ever made a mistake, or that he has any weaknesses. In other words he needs you to make him feel like a god.

So do it. Tell him how masterfully he handled that meeting. Agree how unreasonable his boss is, and how wrong his colleagues are. Point out that his recent "mistake" was in fact a brilliant and counterintuitive masterstroke that will soon pay dividends. Offer to perform on his behalf the task he finds disagreeable. Provide him with the ammunition he needs to win his political battles.

Can't swallow your pride to that extent? Then the interim life is not for you. It sticks in my throat, too. However, I accept that if I were better at it I might have had (and continue to have) an easier time as an interim.

What should I charge?

How to calculate (and maximise) your daily rate

The first question that anyone considering a break into interim life often asks me is "What should I charge?"

There is a great story about the late 'Red' Adair who made a career out of extinguishing oil and gas well fires, becoming rich and famous in the process. He was asked how he arrived at his apparently extortionate fee rate. *"Oh, that's simple"* said Mr Adair. *"I charge a million dollars a day. But there's a catch. The days start from when the fire started, not when the customer asks me in"*.

His interviewer was stunned: *"How do you justify that?"*

"It's very simple. The longer it takes them to call me, the harder it is to put the fire out."

Wouldn't it be great if we could take a leaf out of Red Adair's book? How nice to tell prospective clients "I charge $3000 a day, backdated from the day you should have sacked my predecessor and called me in…" But obviously we are not all Red Adairs, and few of us are risking life and limb in putting out fires. Nevertheless even we lesser mortals need to charge a fee, and the question arises: "How much?" This is of course an impossible question to answer satisfactorily but I will share my thoughts and experiences with you on this thorny subject.

As an interim you will normally be paid for each full day you work. I have on several occasions agreed to charge clients a fixed fee for a single deliverable piece of work but charging in that way is normally associated with consultancy work rather than interim management. It is also uncommon for interims to be paid by the hour; that is a feature of consultancy work rather than interim management.

In order to win your first interim assignment you will normally need to accept a lower rate than you might wish. Once you've got one successful assignments under your belt your fee rate can start to climb. But take it easy!

A common mistake committed by new interim managers is to charge a fee rate based on what they feel a salaried and benefited employee would be paid, simply calculated pro rata on a daily basis. So for example a £100K permanent job becomes a £500 daily interim rate (£100K divided by 200 days, roughly the number of working days in the year). This is however hopelessly unrealistic. In my view an interim needs to earn significantly more than the salaried and benefited equivalent, for the following reasons:

1. You are of course the best in the business and so worth a premium in any case. (If you are not the best in the business you shouldn't think about becoming an interim - or you should set your sights slightly lower.)

2. As an interim you must budget on the basis that you are going to be out of work for some part of the year. (Interim management doesn't *have* to be like that but realistically that is what you should budget for.) Each assignment finishes with you effectively being made redundant but with no compensation for that redundancy. So you need to be paid more to compensate for that.

3. Being an interim is a hard life; you are always working in a new and unknown organisation, often charged with solving difficult problems caused by failure on the part of your predecessor. Often you are working away from home, or at the end of a difficult commute. This just isn't comparable to life as an employee in a steady-state environment, where frankly for much of the time you are just minding the shop.

4. Interims are not entitled, and rarely receive, bonuses for a job well done in the way that senior employees are often rewarded. So an interim's fee rate needs to have the bonus built in; as we said before, you are the best in the business, and you do of course anticipate solving the client's problems...

Depending on what field you are in there may be a market rate for the kind of work you do, particularly if you operate in a well-developed field such as IT contracting, or in the public sector. If this is the case then no matter how good you are, you are going to struggle to lift your rate above the norm. To achieve a higher rate you need to change your offering so that you no longer operate in that market. By working in more specialist fields where you are one of only a few operators it will be easier to set the rate you want.

Some interim agencies work on the "1% rule", although this is increasingly seen as rather an old-fashioned approach. By this they mean that the interim is paid a daily fee of 1% of the annual salary that the role would pay a full-time employee. So, for example, an interim would get paid £1000 per day for a £100K role. (The agency would actually charge the client more than that, the difference being their profit margin.) If you are new to the game of interim management this is not a bad starting point, and it has at least the validity of being based on the hard reality of the permanent salary. My approach is different; I try to value the job and price accordingly.

I am reluctant to suggest a fee rate until I have talked to the client and gained some understanding of the role and the commitment I am being asked to make. My fee rate depends on a wide range of factors, such as the degree of responsibility I am being asked to accept, the length of the contract, the notice period on either side, the type of role and the degree of support I am going to get, the objectives for the role, the geographical convenience of the assignment, etc. Clients normally understand this, and by explaining to my prospective client the issues that influence my fee rate I enter into a useful dialogue that helps me to gain an understanding of the client's problem, and show my empathy for that problem. The objective whenever a client approaches me is to gain an opportunity to meet them and discuss their problem, and a discussion regarding fee rates follows on from this quite naturally.

Nevertheless clients and agencies will often press me to know what my "normal" or "standard" fee rate is. I usually respond by explaining briefly the issues that influence the rate I charge, and providing them with a range.

You should not allow the fee rate you have charged previous clients to be used as a guide for what you should charge prospective new clients. You are perfectly at liberty to suggest a higher rate where you feel it is justified; avoid being type-cast as a "$1000 per day man". The fee rate for your last assignment is unlikely to be relevant to any discussion about the fee rate for a new, and different, assignment. If pressed, by all means tell them but explain the differences between that role and the one now being discussed and emphasise that it is not necessarily realistic to compare the fee rates.

Not surprisingly my fee rate also depends hugely upon whether I want to do the work or not. A short, well-defined and interesting assignment for a client that will add value to my CV will find me quite good value. A client offering an assignment of undefined length and vague objectives, in a dreary town a long journey away, will find me more expensive.

A useful lesson is to know is that if the client is interested in you - the interest usually having been generated by meeting you - but your suggested fee rate is too high, he will normally ask you to reduce it to what he feels is reasonable rather than simply write you off. Successful interims tend to operate in fields where there is not much competition, and the chances of another interim having your precise skills *and being available* are usually small. So there is nothing to lose by suggesting a higher rate; better to start high and come down, rather than start low and get stuck there! And indeed, the negotiating process helps you demonstrate knowledge of your own worth, an understanding of the scale of the task, and an ability to handle yourself calmly when under pressure. A good negotiator will enhance, rather than damage, his credibility. I can say with absolute confidence that I have never, not once, lost a job I wanted because my quoted fee rate was too high, although I have on occasions been asked to accept a lower rate. Sometimes I have agreed, and sometimes I have stuck to the quoted rate.

Here is another useful tip when negotiating with a client who is being rather miserly about the fee rate: It is not uncommon for interims to set a lower fee rate for an assignment of a defined period, and to word the contract such that the fee rate for any days provided beyond that initial period will be subject to renegotiation. Clients often agree to this because they are optimistic about the length of time they will need the interim for, and the interim is assured that he is not committing him or herself to a lengthy assignment at a fee rate lower than he or she would like. When the time comes for extending the contract you have the whip hand; it is going to be very difficult for the client to find someone else to replace you, and he really has no choice but to accept whatever fee rate you can reasonably suggest.

One of my frustrations in my line of work is that I regularly find myself negotiating a fee rate for a role that has been hopelessly undervalued by the client firm. It often doesn't occur to the firm that that's why they lost the guy they now need to replace: If he was good, he left because he wasn't being paid enough. If he was bad, they sacked him without it occurring to them that the reason they are didn't have a good guy in place is because the salary they are offering is not sufficient to attract someone of decent calibre. Organisations can get themselves into a spiral of failure in this way and it often takes a really good interim solution to show them the value they could gain from offering a decent salary to a high-quality individual.

You should normally bill your client each month. Billing on a weekly basis is for temporary clerical staff. Some interims prefer to bill fortnightly on the basis that it is easier for both you and your client to remember what you have done over the last two, rather than last four, weeks. Nevertheless I prefer monthly billing; it is the way in which a professional services firm operates and it keeps the paperwork within reasonable bounds. Needless to say I keep an impeccable daily record of hours / days worked and billable expenses incurred (my A4 notebook again) that my excellent Company Secretary Vicky has no difficulty in converting into a prompt monthly invoice.

If you find work via an agency you must expect them to get involved in the discussion around what fee is appropriate but my advice is to take no nonsense from them. The agency will take their cut from the daily rate you charge, and it is normal for your invoices to go the agency, which then invoices the client at a higher rate. In this situation your contract will normally be between the agency and your own company, rather than directly with the client.

Success fees

I know that some interims negotiate bonuses payable on the achievement of agreed and measurable objectives. I have never done this because success in my field is very difficult to measure empirically and is too open to debate, but good luck to those who can achieve this. If you operate in a field where success can be measured using hard figures it may be worth raising this in your initial discussion with your potential client. Many organisations are receptive to the idea of paying an interim for successful delivery, rather than just for days and hours worked; it shows at least that you are results-focused, which is the most powerful attribute of any successful interim manager. Even just suggesting that fees are paid in this way could help you win the business where you are in competition with other potential interim candidates for the role, even where you eventually agree a fixed daily rate and no success fee; at least you have had a discussion with the client about the objectives and priorities he has in mind. Empathy with the client's problem is a key step to getting the gig.

The contractual arrangements in these types of agreement normally allow for a daily fee rate to be paid for the duration of the assignment, with an agreed final bonus to be paid at the successful end of the assignment.

Expenses

If the assignment is going to involve a lot of travel you need to understand whether (if at all) your out-of-pocket expenses are going to be met before you accept the job. If they are not, you have to decide whether the agreed fee rate is sufficient. An old school friend of mine operated for several years as a self-employed trouble-shooter in the food industry (which is by the way a fantastic industry to get into as an interim; it's an industry that can't stand still for a moment). His work involved frequent travel to food factories across the UK and northern Europe. He nearly always agreed an expenses-included fee rate and met his travelling and accommodation needs with an old camper van, thereby boosting his income quite substantially by the amount he saved on hotel bills. He's an old hippy and it's a life that suited him. Some interims of my acquaintance agree a daily fee which includes the cost of a fancy hotel, and then book into the local B&B, which can also be very soothing for the pension fund.

Make sure that you understand your client's policies with regard to expenses, and before you buy that business-class ticket!

One point worth mentioning with regard to the UK is that some firms, particularly those that operate in the financial services sector, and most public organisations, have difficulty in reclaiming the VAT you are forced to charge them. As you are required to pay VAT on most of the expenses you incur, and then add a further 17.5% before billing your client, this can be expensive for your client. A simple way around this problem is for your expenses to be paid directly by the client firm; costs such as hotel bills, train and plane tickets etc, can normally be settled in this way, avoiding the need for the client to pay VAT on top of VAT. This works in many other countries too.

Getting started as an interim

So you've decided to give the interim game a go?

The first step is to establish a limited liability company. This is quite easily achieved by buying an off-the-shelf company from the many web sites that offer this service. It really doesn't matter what the company is called; you can change it later if required, or use a trading name, but make sure the trading name you choose isn't already licensed to another firm. A useful tip is to buy a company with a relatively recent inception date that you can then state as the first day of trading; this makes the accounting easier at year end.

A limited company is essential in this business because it ensures that if a client does sue, they are suing the firm that employs you as a director, not you and your personal assets. It also makes life much easier by keeping your personal finances separate from your business finances, something your accountant will thank you for. It helps too to establish you in the eyes of HM Revenue & Customers as a contractor rather than as an employee, thereby avoiding tax complications and contractual difficulties for your client. And finally, a limited company is a normal requirement for anybody operating as a professional; clients will demand it.[4]

---

[4] Although in recent times some UK clients (particularly those in the public sector) have become wary about taking on interims as self-employed people due to Inland Revenue pressure to prove that the self-employment is genuine. For most interim engagements the demonstration is easy enough but where the engagement is lengthy and open-ended, and you are taking a management position (which is normally the case) it can be a good idea to discuss with the client firm the alternative option of a temporary or fixed-term employment contract. This issue is changing almost daily as the UK government considers the boundaries between employment and self-employment, prompted by the emerging 'gig economy'. To find out more enter 'IR35' into any internet search engine.

Choosing a name for your business is an important decision. As a self-employed person there is no reason why you shouldn't just use your own name or initials; "Gordon Consulting" for example, or AG Consulting". A business name that hints at what you do isn't a bad notion but avoid allowing yourself to be too typecast, and don't choose anything cheesy: "Risk Management-R-Us" would not have endeared me to my clients and would no doubt have prompted a less than charming letter from the legal representatives of a certain chain of toy shops. And remember that whatever name you choose you've got to be able to phone people and say "Hi! This is Andy of.....". You need to be able to do this and keep a straight face, and you don't want a name that no-one can catch until it's spelt out to them letter by letter. (For this reason avoid the modern and rather silly trend towards numerals and punctuation marks.)

Your limited company will need to be set up with you as a director and shareholder. You will also need to appoint a Company Secretary. This can be your spouse or partner if you like but throughout my self-employed career I have employed the services of a wonderful lady who operates as a professional bookkeeper and secretary, Vicky. Vicky has full authority to sign things on my behalf, which makes life easier for me. (I have already explained that one of my key goals is a life as uncomplicated as possible.) Vicky's address is also my business address so that all those kind letters from the VATman, the taxman and the bank go to her to sort out. And all the bills, fee cheques, etc.

In the UK you will need to apply for VAT authorisation. I don't need to explain how to do this; HM Customs & Excise's own guidance makes this very simple. (I assume here that your anticipated fee earnings will take you over the annual VAT threshold.) You can of course trade before you receive a VAT number but if you bill any clients before this is received you have to either:

a) bill them for VAT on an invoice without a VAT number and promise to forward the VAT number once received, or

b) bill without VAT until the VAT number is received and then bill them again for the VAT element.

Either option is messy and reminds your client that you are a new business, which isn't good for your image or your ability to demand those high fee rates.

Then you need to apply for a bank account. It must be a business bank account, and my advice is to approach a bank that offers free business banking as long as you are not overdrawn. As an interim management business you are unlikely to be overdrawn, so why pay bank charges?

Next, you need to inform the Revenue of your new business' existence. You don't need to worry about this straight away because the taxman will write to you soon enough asking for details of the business. He's very endearing that way.

Then you need to find an accountant. The best way to do this is by personal recommendation from someone whose judgement you trust. In my case the wonderful Vicky recommended a firm she has dealt with for years for her other clients and I am glad I took her advice. You need an accountant that is scrupulously honest (I hope this goes without saying) and who will proactively suggest the most tax advantageous ways of achieving what you need to achieve in terms of meeting your financial commitments and paying yourself a decent wage. I prefer my arrangements in this regard to be as plain and as straightforward as possible. In my case my accountant has set up a PAYE scheme for me, augmented by dividend payments as I when I feel I need the money and my business can afford it. This means I receive a fixed amount each month which is enough to keep the wolf from the door, and any surplus at the end of the year is paid as a final dividend, if I need it. It works for me.

You will probably need some form of business insurance. In my line of work as a consultant to the financial services industry professional indemnity (PI) insurance is essential and I carry £1M worth of cover. (Be warned; PI cover can be appallingly expensive; my annual premium in the first year I traded was over £4000 but over the years it has reduced by half as the insurers see me as a more reliable risk.) Depending on your line of work you may also need some public liability cover; talk to a good broker and take his advice about what your business needs.

These simple steps will take up to six weeks, depending on how busy the VATman is. It is therefore an excellent idea to set up your new business before you start your first interim assignment.

How to write a CV that will get you interim work

Finally but most importantly, you need a CV. An interim manager lives and dies by his or her reputation, and by the quality of his or her CV. Your CV is the most important marketing tool you have and it is absolutely vital that you maintain and nurture it. I am not in this book going to tell you how to write a CV - there are lots of books you can buy that contain that advice - but I am going to give you some tips about how to write a CV that will help you win interim management assignments:

The CV should wherever possible describe your past career successes in evidential and empirical (i.e. measurable) terms. Vague boasts such as "I significantly reduced the department's budget" isn't good enough; you need to say that "I reduced the department's headcount by 20% and its salary budget by 55%" or "the new product line I and my team launched increased top-line revenue by 63% and profits by 34%". Words like "drastically", "significantly" and "major improvement" are okay but figures are better - they speak for themselves without the need to make boastful claims that no-one is going to pay any attention to anyway. Just give me the facts, ma'am, just give me the facts...

Show that you achieved the objectives the organisation set for you. Prospective clients want to be assured that you are a problem solver, someone who focuses on what is important. The CV should not just say what you think you are good at.

Try to avoid making the CV sound like you alone solved the organisation's problems. Most business solutions require teamwork, and your prospective client will want to know that you are a team player.

The prospective client will also want assurance that when the interim assignment comes to an end his own staff will be able to handle the problem for themselves. So your CV should where possible show that you have successfully handed over management responsibilities to client colleagues or a good successor. If during a previous interim assignment you helped the client find a permanent replacement for you, make that clear; a prospective client will welcome assurance that you are willing and able to find a permanent solution to his or her problems.

Your CV must <u>not</u> refer to your fee rate. That is for negotiation once the client has agreed that he would like to hire you.

If you have some interim or consultancy experience your CV should wherever possible contain plaudits from previous happy clients. If you don't have their permission for this, either get their permission, or as a last resort quote them anonymously. Attributable praise from past clients is absolutely priceless. (I discuss later in this book how to get agreement from clients to be quoted in this way.)

Your CV should be adapted to the prospective client's situation. This is why I like to talk to my potential clients as soon as possible and preferably before they have seen my CV. I can then draft my CV to emphasise the experiences I have that directly relate to their particular problem. I've done most things in my line of work; it's just a case of highlighting what is relevant.

Taking control of your finances

I am convinced that people who are attracted to interim management have different values to the rest, and one of the ways this difference manifests itself is the interim's attitude to money. For me, and for the many other interims I have as friends, money is just a way of storing up credit that can be spent on buying free time. Interims are not motivated by status; the 'executive' house, the swanky car and the expensive holidays have little appeal; they are just ways of frittering away your precious free time credit and forcing you to work harder for longer. Having money in the bank is tremendously liberating; it allows you to say "no" to jobs that don't appeal.

My wife and I have paid off the mortgage and reduced our lifestyle (or rather reduced the cost of our lifestyle) to the extent that we can get by quite comfortably, without having to make any significant changes to our lives or enjoyments, on a combined net income of about £24,000, or £12,000 each. With the current tax regime of the UK this requires a gross income of about £17,000 gross each. (Take my word for it, we have done the sums.) Well, I can, and normally do, earn £17,000 in the first few weeks of an assignment. In theory then I could work say one month a year and take it easy for the other eleven months. Of course interim assignments are not normally that short, six months is the usual minimum. But that's fine; the excess I make over my lifestyle needs just brings the day I retire and live the life of Riley ever closer[5].

The excess earnings over lifestyle needs has also allowed me to build up quite a substantial buffer fund. An obvious risk of interim life is that you may find yourself out of work for some of the time. Hopefully these periods will be short but you need to budget on them being longer than you would wish. When I left the happy shiny world of permanent employment I had some savings that I could have drawn upon if required, and I augmented this as soon as I could to build up a fund that would see me through twelve months without fresh income, if necessary. Thankfully I have never had to draw upon it to that extent but it is reassuring to know it's there. It makes me more ready to turn down those assignments that stink, and more confident when negotiating my fee rates with new potential clients; if

---

[5] In fact, as I write this, that day has nearly arrived. It's just over the next hill...

it's not what I want, I can afford to wait for a more suitable opportunity.

But when you make the decision to become self-employed it pays to consider what you are going to lose by switching from the cosy world of employment; the company pension, death-in-service benefits, the private health plan, the company car and subsidised mortgage, etc. You should take this opportunity to review your finances and to establish what you are going to need as a self-employed person. A principle concern for me when I went self-employed was life insurance and permanent health insurance (PHI). Life insurance so that if anything happened to me my wife could still cope financially, and PHI so that if I suffered a serious illness or injury and was unable to work, we could still manage. I also bought some critical illness insurance for the same reasons.

PHI is expensive but the trick is to determine how long you could manage financially without receiving any fee income (i.e. the length of time your buffer fund would last) and setting the deferment period - the length of time you have to wait before the monthly cheques start to arrive from the insurance company - to that length of time. In my case I arranged things so we could survive for a year without an income (my buffer fund again) and set the deferred period at that. I also set the amount I needed to receive if unable to work to as low as a reasonable lifestyle could demand; in this way I have kept the premium within reasonable bounds.

A pension scheme is essential but the only advice I can give you here is to seek professional advice. By professional I mean avoiding the salesmen; you need to find a good-quality independent financial adviser, preferably one who charges a fee for his time rather than take commission from the products he sells.

As a self-employed person you are only a missed heartbeat away from having no income at all. So do the sensible thing and make provision.

The tools of the interim trade

A laptop is essential. It doesn't have to be an expensive one; mine cost less than £400 and I chose it because it's small, light and easy to carry. You need the right software; Microsoft Office or some software that is compatible with it, is essential so that you have or can at least use documents written in Microsoft Word, PowerPoint, Excel and Outlook; these are the basic business languages of the professional world. Any software requirements over and above this will depend on the business you are in, and I can't help you there.

You need an email address. You *must* buy a domain so that you can have an email address that contains your business name thereby avoiding the likes of gmail, hotmail, etc. You must also avoid twee, cheesy or jokey email addresses; you need a professional image and no-one is going to put their business problems in the hands of jenniesbestestmummy1986@gotmail.com or the like.

A business card is essential. It should be plain and simple; your name, email address and phone numbers. Don't include your home address if it's the kind of address that would make it obvious that you are working from home; no 'proper' business is run from Acacia Avenue. You can let the client know where to send the money once you have won the work, so don't worry about that. Another solution is to follow my example and make your business address the address of your book-keeper. The wonderful Vicky has a much more business-appropriate address than I do, and it also ensures that she gets all the mail and not me.

Your business card and office stationery should *not* refer to any particular trade, profession or specialism. You want to keep your options open rather than allow yourself to be typecast, and you need a business card that is transferable across industries and disciplines. And don't put a job title on the card either; no-one is going to be impressed that you are a "Managing Director" or "President" or whatever.

67

Unless all of your assignments can be reached by public transport, and assuming you drive, you will need a car. It doesn't have to be an expensive one; turning up in flashy motor isn't going to help you win the work or endear you to the already wary client staff. Nor should it be ludicrously cheap and shabby; a client wants to feel that his business problems are in the hands of someone who is financially successful. A smart but low-key car is perfect. (And please; no personalised number plates; they are just too estate agent.) An expensive car is also silly way of burning a lot of hard-earned cash. Put the money to better use and build up your buffer fund, and then get rid of your mortgage, and then feed your pension. Take control of your life, rather than allowing your need for money to control you - this for me is what the interim life is all about.

A mobile phone (cellphone in the US) is obviously essential. Cheesy ring-tones should be avoided.

Finally, buy a new suit (this goes for the women too!), some new shirts or blouses, polish your shoes, get your hair cut / done, and if you are overweight, lose the extra pounds. This may sound unduly harsh and fattist but there is no doubt - and plenty of evidence to prove - that clients are much more likely to buy professional services from someone who looks like he or she has looked after him or herself. Buyers make subconscious and even conscious connections about smartness, fitness, self-control and competence. This may not be fair but it is reality; get over it.

How to find interim assignments

Here are the ways in which interims normally find their work: From their own network of friends and business contacts, from agencies, from direct approaches to potential clients, and via LinkedIn and other networking websites.

Here are some ways in which you are very unlikely to find interim assignments:

- From the impressive website you have spent weeks in setting up.

68

- From the marketing material that looks so pretty and which cost you a small fortune to design and print.

By all means spend time and money developing a website and marketing material but don't expect it to find you so much as a day's work. It might help you impress a potential client (particularly if you are offering yourself as an interim designer of websites or marketing materials) but it is unlikely to help you find the client and get in front of him.

As I write this I have no website or marketing materials. I never have. I just have a decent LinkedIn profile[6], a business card and some matching stationery designed by a friend of mine who used to be a professional commercial artist, and I have had as much work as I want. Most of my past clients have come to me because they know me, or because we have a mutual acquaintance who has recommended me, or because they have found me via LinkedIn. My experience is that all successful interims are excellent networkers, and this takes time and effort. I have an address book with about the names of about 350 business contacts, 100 of whom get an email or phone call from me at least annually, and some more often that that. I will normally have lunch or a drink with half a dozen of them a month. It's hard work but well worth it; most of my assignments have come to me this way. Clients like giving work to people they know; it makes them feel good to be able to say to their colleagues: *"I had lunch last month with a guy who does that kind of thing. I'll give him a call and see if he's available"*.

Networking is not just about stroking potential clients. An interim who specialises in a particular industry or discipline will normally find that he operates in a small world where everyone knows everyone else. By networking you will be keeping an ear to the ground; finding out about firms in trouble, firms who have lost an

---

[6] Even this is now a shadow of its former self. When it's too rich I get pestered!

incumbent, and firms who are planning a major project; all may be in the market for an interim.

Don't be afraid of contacting firms to offer your services as an interim even when they are advertising for a permanent employee. Senior managers can take a very long time to replace; advertising a vacancy, selecting candidates for interview, interviewing them (often more than once, with an "assessment day" in between), negotiating their package, and waiting for them to work out their notice period (normally at least three months these days) can take up to a year. This protracted process is one of the key reasons why the interim management market is growing so quickly. So firms can be receptive to the idea of an interim manager, even where that solution had not occurred to them until your charming letter and interesting CV arrived on their desk (or even better, when they picked up your phone call). If you can find out who the hiring firm is, go direct to them rather than to the recruitment agency they are hiding behind. (Finding out this kind of thing is why maintaining your network is so important; it gives you access to that kind of inside information.)

Some of my work has come via agencies. I don't mind finding work this way; agencies seem prepared to pay me the same fee rates that I charge when contracting direct to clients. But see my comments above about agencies - I have yet to come across an agency that adds any real value to the interim/client relationship. Despite the agencies' claims most are simply acting as middlemen and taking their margin in return for effecting an introduction. Someone has to do it, I suppose.

Undoubtedly the biggest change that has happened during my interim career has been the increasing importance of, and power of, the internet as a silent middleman between clients and interims. I have found projects by conducting relevant searches of various job websites - there are some that specialise in contract roles - and clients have found me via my LinkedIn profile. I strongly advise that you take time to set up a strong LinkedIn profile that contains the relevant words and phrases that will act as a catch to anyone seeking someone with your skills. If you are not sure about how to go about designing a good profile get advice and support from someone you trust.

How to avoid overstaying your welcome

Successful interims will find that their assignments are often extended beyond the initially agreed duration. It is by no means unusual for three or six month contracts turn into year-long marathons. This happens for a number of reasons:

a) The client under-estimates the length of time it takes to find and install an employed replacement for the role currently occupied by the interim;

b) Projects take longer than anticipated to complete, or suffer from 'scope creep';

c) The client gets used to the interim being around and finds it comforting. As time goes by the need to find an employee to fill the interim's role somehow seems less urgent. Other more immediately pressing problems demand management's attention;

d) Even when a suitable employee is found, the client often likes the interim to stick around to provide a hand-over period;

e) Once an interim has a good relationship with his client it is amazing how often the client will put the interim's name forward as someone to run the next project. Trust is an important factor.

All very satisfying and a common feature of a successful interim's working life. It is twenty times easier to win work from an existing client than it is to win work from a new client but accept some words of caution from a battle-hardened veteran of the game:

A good interim will always ensure that his relationship with the client is kept within professional bounds and that his 'critical success factors' (I apologise for lapsing into consultancy jargon for a moment) are identified and monitored. In other words, an interim is there to do a job, and he will ensure that the 'job' is clearly defined, and that he is seen as having completed it to the full satisfaction of his client. In this way his reputation is grown, his marketability improved, and his fee rate for the next interim role maximised. A good interim has a CV which is a hard, unequivocal record of success at each assignment.

Allowing an interim assignment to drift away from those clear objectives that were set at the start of the job is to risk this process going astray. The interim and the client forget what it was that he (the interim) was there to achieve. New objectives are brought in which blur the successful achievement of the original objectives. The critical success factors are forgotten, and the interim's performance of them overlooked.

There is also a risk that no matter how good your performance in the initial project or role, if you are not seen as being so successful in your new project or role, the client's memory of you, his perception of your abilities and how well you succeeded, will be damaged by your performance in the second assignment, to the detriment of your CV and your reputation.

Having said all this it is absolutely the case that the easiest way to find work as an interim is by selling your ongoing services to your current client. The alternative - getting work from a new client - is much harder. But if you are offered another position by an existing client make sure that it suits you and your abilities. Is it really you? Does it play to your strengths? Or are you taking something on that is outside your area of expertise and which will expose your weaknesses? Would it be better if you just moved on, took some time off, and started afresh on new ground?

If you decide to take another assignment from your current client, apply the same discipline that you would for a new client. Establish clear objectives and performance measurements. Before taking it on ask the client for a critique of your performance in the first assignment. Get those words of glowing praise agreed here and now; if you leave it until the second project has completed the client will have forgotten how well you did - particularly if the second project bombs.

Also ask yourself whether the new assignment justifies an enhanced fee rate. There is no reason why the fee rate for the first assignment should automatically apply to the second. One point worth remembering is that it is easier to negotiate a better rate if you have another potential client lined up, and all good interims try to achieve this as they come to the end of an assignment.

This leads me to another point: If you are successful as an interim you will often find that at any one time (but particularly towards the end of a client contract) you will have a number of irons in the fire, i.e. new potential client opportunities pressing you for commitment. By allowing yourself to get involved in another assignment with your current client are you turning down other opportunities for career development, CV improvement or (most importantly) fee enhancement?

A good interim assignment is one in which the duration is agreed at the outset, the objectives and critical success factors established, and the assignment is completed to the client's full satisfaction. The interim leaves when his contract expires, his reputation sky-high. You go in, you do the job and you leave to go to the next job. Your clients talk about you in the warmest terms to other potential clients (and are happy to act as referees).

There is no doubt that as an interim you can overstay your welcome. Employees can begin to resent the fact that you "always seem to be around" and that you "always get the plum jobs". They know what fee rate you are on - they always find *that* out - and they will compare it to their own small (by comparison) salaries. When you arrived you were an unknown and impressive operator but now, after they've got to know you, they have seen that you're just a mere mortal like them. ("Who does he think he is? - God's gift or something?") You will know when it's time to go. It will be after you have achieved your objectives and given your client a permanent solution to his problem but before you've become part of the furniture.

Getting your invoices paid

Only once has it happened to me that one of my bills has not been paid. It was relatively early in my interim career, and like many appalling experiences it provided a very valuable lesson which I pass on to you, Dear Reader, so that you can avoid making the same stupid mistakes as me:

I was engaged to a well-known insurance company but contracted via an agency that was new to me. The insurance company client was an excellent firm I wanted to work for, and the assignment was reasonably well paid and interesting. Unfortunately the agency with whom I was contracted went bust after a couple of months into the assignment. As I was to discover later its owner had taken far too much out of the business to fund a lavish and unrealistic lifestyle, and my fee, along with a lot of other money that did not properly belong to him, was blown on his collection of Ferraris. The insurance company had paid the agency but the agency had not paid me. It wasn't just the fee for the work I had done, either; I had incurred significant hotel and travel expenses which I was not able to recover.

To say I was furious would be an understatement. I will never forget the dreadful sick feeling in my stomach when I realised that I had sweated for a month for an agency who was unlikely, and probably unable, to pay my bill, and that the thousands I had incurred in hotel and travel expenses would not be reimbursed.

I was naïve, and should have seen the warning signs. The agency did not have a good reputation, and was not a member of the Interim Management Association or associated with the Institute of Interim Management. It had little experience of acting as an interim agency; most of its income came from one-off recruitment fees for permanent employees. And crucially, when it contracted me, it had insisted on a 40-day payment period, so that my invoices were not paid until 40 days after they were received by the agency, even though I knew that the agency was billing the insurance client on a 30-day payment period. In other words my fees were being used to support the agency's cash flow and reduce its overdraft. It had also made a lot of people redundant recently; this alone should have warned me that it was on its last legs.

Of course, I should not have agreed to such payment terms, and the fact that the agency had asked for them should have been sufficient warning to steer clear of the contract. All reputable interim agencies will pay the interim on a 30-day payment period (assuming a monthly billing cycle) and you should be very wary of any firm which asks you to agree to a different arrangement. If client firms are slow to pay the agency it is the agency's cash flow that should bear the strain, not the interim's. This is well understood by all reputable agencies who ensure that their business is capitalised appropriately.

So if you are contracting via an agency, check it out. How long has it been in the interim market, and what is its reputation? Is it a member of the Interim Management Association? Use your contacts to see whether it has any history of failure to pay promptly, or any other issues that give rise to concern.

Depending on how successful your interim career has been to date, and how optimistic you are about the prospect of other work, you may feel that it is worth the risk of contracting via an agency for whom you do not have absolute confidence. There are ways in which you can mitigate the risk:

- Insist on a short billing cycle - even weekly if necessary - and very prompt payment terms, so that if the agency does fail it will not take a whole month's income from you.

- If you can, agree a late payment interest penalty clause in your contract. (I have on many occasions slipped this into my contract without the client or agency even noticing. If clients check the contract at all it is by passing it to their legal departments, and lawyers are used to such terms appearing in supplier contracts.)

- Try to make arrangements for some or all hotel expenses to be paid directly by the agency, even if it is only the basic room rate. (As discussed earlier this is actually a very good way of reducing both the agency's and the client's costs: If you bill expenses to the agency you have to put VAT of 17.5% on top of the hotel's bill, and the agency then has to put another 17.5% on top of that before billing the client. I always suggest direct billing arrangements to my clients as a way of avoiding this double whammy.)

- Ensure that the agency's contract does not try to pass on to you the risk of the client defaulting. All reputable agencies will carry this risk themselves and protect the interim; this is after all one of the key benefits of contracting via an agency.

- Whatever billing cycle you agree, make sure your invoices are submitted the minute they are due. Even bill in advance if necessary, and submit your invoices via email so that they arrive with the agency immediately rather than get delayed by the post.

- Whenever you can insist on settlement of your bills by direct bank transfer, rather than by cheque, so that the money leaves their account and hits yours as soon as possible.

- Monitor settlement of your bills. If an agency (or a client, if you are billing the directly) does not meet your payment terms and is even one day late, contact them immediately to find out why and to apply pressure. Get the name of whoever is responsible for authorising payment; this will often be your client boss, and you will of course have taken care to ensure that his authorisation has been obtained. Also find out who in the Finance Dept. who will actually pay it. Accept no excuses for late payment.

- If you have managed to insert a late payment interest clause in your contract send them an addition invoice for the penalty interest straight away. Even if they decline to pay the interest it should galvanise them into paying the original invoice, and show them you mean business.

- If payment is still not forthcoming, talk to your boss and explain that if payment is not received by a certain date, you will be forced to down tools. Start making arrangements for this to happen; cancel meetings arranged for after your deadline date. This approach is relevant even if it is the agency that has not paid your bill rather than the client, because if you threaten to leave unless you get paid the client will put pressure on the agency to pay you.

- On one occasion, when dealing with an agency who repeatedly failed to pay me by the due date, I made alternative contractual arrangements directly with the client on the basis that my contract with the agency had been voided. The client was as fed up with the agency's incompetence as I was and was grateful for an opportunity to avoid paying the agency's margin. When the agency threatened legal action against both myself and the client - something to which only a desperate agency would resort - we stood our ground; the agency knew that its record of late payment made its legal case hopeless. It backed down.

Getting paid is one issue that an employee rarely has to worry about but it is an important feature of the interim life. You should not be ashamed about chasing the cash, particularly if the money is owed by an agency. If the money is owed by the client and you are worried that it might damage your relationship with them, get your Company Secretary or book-keeper (or someone you can nominate as such, for this purpose) to do the chasing for you, so that you can detach yourself from the process to some extent. My wonderful Company Secretary Vicky is an excellent credit controller, and if she rubs late-payers up the wrong way from time to time I just shrug my shoulders and say that she is just doing her job.

I always recall the effort that was put into chasing payment by my former 'Big Four' consultancy employers: We had a team of very aggressive lawyers on permanent stand-by who had absolutely no shame in bludgeoning clients for money. Yet their efforts never seemed to affect the relationship we consultants had with the client.

The mistake I describe above that led to my invoice not getting paid was to trust an agency that was not trustworthy. In fact I have never experienced a client not paying my bill. Clients defaulting is a much smaller risk than agencies defaulting; clients who hire interims tend to be of a size such that sudden financial collapse is unlikely, and clients in financial difficulties do not normally hire expensive interims. If clients are reluctant to pay your bill, it is normally because:

- Your contract, and in particular your fee rate, has been agreed by someone who did not have authority to agree it;

- The client thinks you have charged them for time you did not spend, or for expenses you have not incurred or which they do not feel should be borne by them;

- Your performance has been so bad that they consider you to have reneged on your contractual commitments.

You don't need me to tell you how to avoid these mistakes.

If normal pressure for payment does not work:

I once did some work for a well-known life assurer. Life assurers by their nature tend to have a lot of disgruntled customers; life assurance products are complicated promises, promises which, in the eyes of some customers, are not always kept. Most aggrieved customers resort to the normal complaint process, with ultimate recourse to the independent Financial Ombudsman if they don't get satisfaction. Not one canny customer though: He simply turned up one fine Friday afternoon in a large van of the type often referred to in the US as a

'Recreational Vehicle' which he parked across the exit from the executive staff car park. He put the kettle on.

He had his grievance settled within the hour[7].

Other tips for successful interim management

Be fair

In developing your relationships with the client team that report to you, don't have favourites. Inevitably, some of the team given to you will be better than others but don't allow your regard for those individuals to become obvious; the rest of the team will resent it. It is of course right and proper to reward merit but the rewards should be given for proven competence and results, not just because you like the person, or because they remind you of you at a younger age.

Keep it professional

Don't get romantically (to use a euphemism) involved with any of the client staff. This advice falls into the 'bleeding obvious' category, I know, but time and time again I see interims losing their relationship with the client, their hard-won respect, and sometimes their assignment, because word has got round that the interim is romantically involved with someone in the firm. It really is surprisingly common. If either of the parties are already married (to other people!) it's appallingly messy but even genuine and serious relationships do damage. Don't assume that your office romance will be looked on indulgently by everyone else; it won't. And don't be so naïve as to assume that it will be kept a secret; such relationships never are. If you really feel you are falling for someone in the client firm my only advice (and I speak as someone to whom this has never happened or, I hasten to add, is ever likely to happen) is to either end the relationship, or end the client assignment, as quickly as possible.

---

[7] I'm not recommending this approach. Just admiring of it.

Your reputation as a professional will be damaged if you allow the relationship to develop whilst you are there, in a way in which it will be very difficult to repair.

You may think that this is an unlikely risk but I have seen many promising interim and consultancy careers damaged in this way. It's not just the men, either. Perhaps it is a feature of the life of middle-aged, professional and personally impressive people who find themselves for the first time away from their spouse or partner, surrounded by people who are slightly in awe of them?

Expect the unexpected

Any organisation that has decided to use an interim manager has done so because it has a specific problem. I have already discussed how the problem described to you as your challenge can often prove rather different from the problem that actually exists. You should not be surprised if the problem you are asked to solve proves to be only a small part of a bigger problem, nor should you be surprised if other, newer, problems emerge during your assignment.

Keeping your eyes open for this kind of thing is an important way in which you can identify other opportunities to extend your brief and/or the timescale of your assignment, if it suits you to do so. Or you may be quite satisfied with the scope of the role you have already got, thank you very much, or you may have other opportunities in the pipeline!

Reinvent yourself!

I am aware that as I have moved from job to job, and now from interim role to interim role, I have been able to develop myself as a person. I have of course gained skills and experience that I have been able to carry forward but something more than that has happened, something that I can't record on a CV: I have been able to leave behind the shy, rather awkward young man from a small northern English town who first started work in an ill-fitting suit. I don't pretend that I have turned into a suave and confident man of the world but there is no doubt that as I have left each employer or client organisation I have been able to leave behind a little bit of myself that was getting in the way of my happiness and success. Maybe a good analogy is that of an actor who, by taking on different roles, avoids being typecast and develops a reputation as a rounded professional but who also extends himself as a person.

The life of an interim gives you plenty of opportunity to become aware of what it is about your personality, your impact on people around you, your emotional strengths and weaknesses, that might be getting in the way of what you want to achieve with your life. Use each new assignment as an opportunity to change, in a small way, what needs to be changed, making gradual and incremental steps. Your resolutions don't have to be major, and in fact are likely to fail if they are; small commitments are all that is required and are more likely to be achieved. It is very difficult for me to give examples because the resolutions will depend on you and your knowledge of yourself. If it helps, I have been aware that I have consciously tried to do more of the following:

- To always use full eye contact whenever I am talking to someone, and to give people my full attention when they are talking to me, no matter how busy and distracted I am;
- To say "thank you" whenever it is appropriate to do so – and even at times when it isn't;
- To give praise whenever the opportunity arises;
- Remember to smile;
- Relax more – remember what's important and what isn't;
- Use humour more often;
- Don't put off phone calls and meetings I know are likely to be unpleasant;
- Favour the phone or a meeting over an email whenever possible;
- If someone disappoints me, to not be afraid to say so, politely but firmly (but especially when I am their customer).

All rather pathetic really but I suspect that someone who knew me well 30 years ago (and I have some very good friends who do) would say that I have changed.

By reinventing yourself, I don't mean trying to become someone you're not. Happiness lies in feeling comfortable about showing the world your real face and not an invented one - but your real face can change. I am convinced that this is one of the advantages of interim management as a career; it accelerates the development of yourself, not just as a technical adviser and manager but as a person.

Know your competition

This is an important factor of any business activity and needs to be taken seriously by interim managers. Few assignments are won without competition. You may think that you are unique, and to be fair you may even *be* unique in the skills and experience you have and the approach you take to client's problems. However, as far as the potential client is concerned you are just one of a number of possible solutions to his problem. So you need to know what you are up against.

In my case I have many competitors. All of the major consultancy firms can offer someone who does (or at least can claim to do) what I do. There seems to be an ever-increasing number of 'boutique' consultancy firms trying to establish themselves too, as the consultancy market grows and fragments. I am also up against all of the other self-employed one-man bands, and they grow in number constantly. You are likely to find yourself in the same position.

I work hard to keep in touch with what my competitors are doing. I regularly meet contacts who work for the firms concerned, or their clients. I make a point of attending breakfast seminars hosted by these firms, or just pop into their reception areas and pinch their marketing material to see what services they are touting this month, and how. (The services are all the same but the bigger firms are good at packaging them in a way which makes them seem new and sexy, even though the basic skills of the management consultant haven't changed since the dawn of time.)

I also buy people lunches. One of Britain's favourite pastimes is talking shop (we should demand it be made an Olympic sport, we would win gold every time) and all I have to do is pour the wine and listen. It's amazing what people will divulge to a sympathetic, discreet and understanding listener. Never underestimate the power of gossip; the City of London (my home territory) runs on it.

Most important of all, I find out what fees my competitors are charging. Under-cutting the major firms is easy - I can charge myself out at half the rate my former employers charged me out at and still make serious money - but I never try to compete against the smaller firms and the one-man bands on price. I am, in comparison to them, a relatively expensive option, and I neither draw attention to this fact nor apologise for it. Clients buy me because I'm the best (or at least the best available at the time!) and not because I'm the cheapest. I can prove I'm the best by showing clients my CV, by putting them in touch with my former clients, and by meeting the client to talk about their problem. I can soon show that the cheaper option could turn out to be very expensive in the long run, although I don't do this by knocking the competition. I do it by asking the client the right questions; questions that disturb them and which get them thinking about their problem in a more realistic and imaginative way.

I have very rarely been asked to reduce my quoted fee rate, and on the few occasions I can recall where this happened I did so by bringing it down to what I had already privately decided was a reasonable fee. I have regularly won work against cheaper opposition. I do this by deliberately differentiating myself from my competitors: I take a different approach to the bigger firms in that I am prepared to stand my ground when dealing with the industry's regulator and the Financial Services Ombudsman, for example, and I have proven success at designing more imaginative and cheaper solutions than you will get from the consultancy firms. I am also willing to help in finding my permanent successor; the consultancy firms don't usually like to get involved in this because it's too high-risk for them. When I'm pitching against the smaller more specialist consultancy firms whose pricing is closer to my own I simply emphasise the depth and breadth of my experience and the fact that I've been doing what I do for some time, with proven results; something the younger firms struggle to demonstrate. So far, touch wood, I have rarely lost an assignment I truly wanted to win, although I have on occasions backed out of competitions for roles I did not want.

Using your down-time wisely

Even the busiest interim will at some time experience gaps between assignments. Sometimes these gaps are voluntary, and sometimes they occur simply because the next assignment doesn't immediately follow the previous one. Whichever is the case these gaps are to me one of the key advantages of interim management as a career option; they give me time to do some things I want to do which I would not be able to squeeze into a career as a permanent employee. Time is the most precious commodity we have; we will all run out of it eventually. So how should you spend it? Here are some ideas:

- By all means take a holiday. You've earned it, and it's hard to take leave when you are on an assignment. But if you haven't already organised the next assignment you should consider first spending some time on finding work. Holidays are much more enjoyable when you can relax knowing that the next role is lined up.

- Improve your skills. Buy some training, take a college course, or even work voluntarily for someone who is prepared to train you in return. Don't be frightened of committing yourself to a longish-term project; if the next role arrives and you need to start on Monday the worst that can happen is that you have to leave the training programme or course early. If you have a hankering to move your career into a different area now is the opportunity to get some training and experience.

- Do something you have always wanted to do. During one break, for instance, I worked for two weeks on a voluntarily basis in a friend's classic car restoration workshop. I gave him some free labour, and some key advice on financial management. (I reduced his overdraft by £10,000 by shrinking his parts inventory and improving his billing system, saving him hundreds of pounds a month in bank charges. Obvious, really.) He paid me in tea you could paint roads with, bacon sandwiches, and some nuggets from a lifetime's experience of keeping old cars on the road. In other periods of downtime I have practically rebuilt our house in the South of France, learned to weld, and oh yes! - written this book. You could learn to play a musical instrument, or sail, or paint, or cook; whatever you fancy.

- Learn a foreign language. With commitment (and depending on the language) this can be done from scratch to a basic command with three months' full-time effort. The tutelage will be expensive and it will be very hard work but what an investment in your life and career!

- Sort out your finances. You have worked hard for your money; make sure it's working hard for you.

- Get to know your family again. One of the biggest risks facing a career-minded person is that they neglect their family, and a break between assignments is a good opportunity to redress the balance.

- Get fit. With the best will in the world it is hard to keep up your personal fitness regime during a demanding interim assignment.

But approach any downtime project in just the same disciplined way you approach a client assignment; identify your objectives, set a timetable, and focus on what you need to do to achieve them. Don't just spend time. Think about how it will look on your CV; it's much more powerful to be able to show that between two interim roles you were doing something positive, rather than simply stating that you were on holiday or just 'resting'.

How to finish an interim assignment

The handover

Not every interim assignment ends with a handover to a successor. Interims that are in charge of projects that reach a natural end simply leave at that point, unless they have found other work at the same firm. But most interim assignments do end this way and you will be expected to make sure that the handover process is successful.

So, the happy day arrives when you can start to relax; your successor has arrived! You might even have helped to find and recruit him. At last, you can begin the process of dumping on him the burden you have so manfully (or womanfully) borne during this grueling assignment. But before you start dumping away let's consider some of the things you need to bear in mind:

You are a hard act to follow. This is only natural; you are the best at what you do, of course, and your reputation at the end of a successful interim assignment is sky-high. And you have been around long enough to get to know the organisation, its people and its issues, whilst your successor knows little or nothing. Try to remember what it was like for you when you began the assignment; it was daunting, and you felt as nervous and as excited as your successor does now. So try to make it easy on your successor. Give him the knowledge you wish you had been given when you started. Introduce him to the team and to your colleagues. Explain how the organisation works and give him the information he needs to understand it. Lay the facts out before him.

I say *facts*, because this bit is important: What you must be wary of is giving your successor the benefit of your opinion on the issues, or on the people, or on the politics. Your successor needs an opportunity to make up his own mind about what needs to be done, and he might have different ideas and priorities, which is not an unhealthy thing. I think this is particularly important where people are concerned. In every assignment of any length there are people who rub me up the wrong way, people whose opinion I do not share, people whom I simply do not like. Nevertheless I try to take people as I find them, and I want my successor to do the same. My opinion of someone is only my opinion, and perhaps the relationship my successor has with that person will be better than the one I had. Certainly I prefer to let that happen rather than sour my successor's opinion of him or her from the start.

Also bear in mind that what you say to your successor, your opinions about someone or something, may find the ear of someone whose ear you would rather it did not find. Don't forget that once you have left the organisation people will feel free to tittle-tattle about you as much as they like and they will not feel under any obligation to keep the information you gave to them in confidence to themselves. Remember: Once you're gone you're history, Sunshine.

By all means try to explain to your successor the political landscape as you see it but be wary, for the reasons given above.

Depending on how long a handover period your client has asked for it sometimes makes sense to agree with your successor a date on which you formally hand over the keys, as it were. For me this is important; I frequently take on personal regulatory responsibility for a firm and I need to agree the point at which I formally pass on that responsibility. I do not want any fudging or any misunderstanding about who has the right to make decisions for which I (or my successor) is responsible. In the past where I have run one-month handover periods my successors have been happy to accept formal responsibility at the halfway point - the middle day of the one month period. Perhaps for you and your line of work this kind of formality will be less important but it often pays to discuss it with your successor.

You also need to bear in mind that your successor will want to make his own mark rather than just tag along like a pet lamb. Give him opportunities to chair meetings (where he is happy to do so) and respond to requests for opinion.

If you have occupied an office invite your successor to make himself at home in it, and move to a desk outside (which is where you should have been all along in my opinion, but each to their own). Give up your car-parking space. Buy him lunch.

I always see my successors as potential clients for consultancy work in the future, and I want to make them feel as grateful to me as I possible can, without being creepy about it. This approach has paid big dividends in my interim career, and I recommend it to you. Don't be arch.

What you must remember to do

Let's say then that you are coming to the end of a successful assignment as an interim. Life feels good, and you are looking for the next project. What do you need to remember to do?

1. Revisit the objectives you were given at the start of the assignment and ensure that you have ticked each of them off. Remind the client of your successful accomplishment of your objectives.

2. Ask the client what future projects they may be planning that you could assist in. Remember that is much easier to win a new assignment from an existing client rather than from a new client;

3. Make sure your address book is up to date with the contact details of the key people in the client firm who will be prepared to act as referee. Check with them that they will be happy to do this;

4. Book a lunch date with those key people for (say) three months' time. If nothing else you will find out what happened after you left (I'm always curious to know this) and networking is a key part of the successful interim's life;

5. Say thank you to everyone whose support you have enjoyed. Invite them out for a farewell lunch or drink (but don't get drunk!);

6. Get those precious references and plaudits. Here's how to do it:

How to get the plaudits you need

This isn't just about stroking your ego. Good feedback from satisfied clients is the life-blood of a successful interim. Nothing, absolutely nothing, is as valuable to your success, and you need to start making suitable arrangements as soon as your assignment starts; leaving it to the end will be too late.

As I have discussed earlier in this book you should within a couple of weeks into a new assignment have agreed some objectives with your client. As far as possible these should be specific and measurable but they can be just a list of achievements, boxes both you and the client will be able to tick at the end of the assignment. As you achieve your objectives during the assignment you should bring this to the attention of your client, perhaps during your weekly one-to-one meetings with him. Towards the end of the assignment you should hold a final meeting - a lunch is always nice - in which you review your objectives, look back on your achievements, and get the client's agreement that you have met all of his requirements of the role; your assignment has been a success. At that point (perhaps when he's just finished his second glass of wine) you should ask the client to write a quick note - an email will do - acknowledging this. Even offer to write it for him. Nag him until he gives it to you.

DO NOT WAIT TO DO THIS UNTIL YOU HAVE LEFT THE ORGANISATION: The day you leave is the day the client will begin to forget who you were and what you did. The only thing he will remember is how expensive you were compared to the guy who has replaced you, and that memory does not encourage kind words.

How to increase your income with other work

Once you build a reputation as a successful interim and develop some strong client relationships you will find that other opportunities to make money start to come your way, opportunities that are not interim management per se but which can grow from your role as an independent interim. You should grab these opportunities by the beard[8] and use them to increase your income even further without the sweat that is involved in full-on interim work.

Consultancy

I have talked in the book about the differences between consultancy and interim management but the main difference is very simple; an interim manager takes responsibility for managing a team of people and becomes an officer of the client firm, and a consultant does not; he is only responsible for the advice he gives.

This distinction is sometimes blurred in situations where a consultancy firm loans an individual on secondment to take a position within the client firm. However you should see the caveats, exclusions and wriggle-room consultancy firms build into their contractual arrangements in this situation to make sure that they cannot be held liable for any action or omission on the part of the secondee. This kind of arrangement is about a million miles away from what I consider to be interim management in which the individual concerned takes the part of the client firm in every way and is more than willing to accept responsibility for his actions.

There is one other important difference between interim work and consultancy; consultancy is in my experience easier and much less stressful. Consultancy is more about analysis and plan formulation

---

[8] (*Do you know this eastern European phrase? *"Opportunities have a bearded chin but are bald behind."* In other words, you can grab opportunities on their way towards you but not once they have passed you by - because there is nothing to grab hold of...)

(which of course interim work also involves) but it doesn't come with all of that back-breaking people management stuff which interim management involves. Don't get me wrong; I like interim work but it is nice to leaven it occasionally with a good bit of consultancy. Extending your services in this way can be a very nice layer of jam on top of the bread that was the interim assignment, and you should seize any opportunity to sell your services as a consultant, where it suits you to do so.

Some clients - I would say the more sensible clients - understand that you don't necessarily get the best advice from the big and established consultancy firms and that there are times when a one-man band such as yourself can offer precisely what the client needs, at a fraction of the cost, and without having to fend off the foot-in-the-door sales techniques that is so depressingly a feature of how the big consultancies work. So do not be shy about touting your services as both an interim and a consultant; consultancy work can be very interesting and rewarding. In my experience it is much easier to sell consultancy services to clients for whom you have done interim work in the past and to whom you have demonstrated your credibility, for obvious reasons.

It is possible to pick up consultancy work from clients with whom you have had no previous relationship but I have to admit that this does not happen nearly as much as I would like. It is curious; client firms are reluctant to give consultancy responsibility to someone they don't know but they will with alacrity give that same person full responsibility as an interim even though the latter is demonstrably the bigger risk for the firm concerned.

Retained work

Some while ago I did do a short piece of consultancy work for a boutique asset manager in the City. I was between interim assignments and I did it as a favour for an agency with whom I have had a strong relationship over the years (there are some good agencies out there) but it was actually quite remunerative and interesting work and it was good for the CV; very good reasons to

91

say 'Yes' to any offer of work.   It ended up as just a month's work in total but my client was delighted with my services; they had been the victim of some advice from a consultancy firm that claims to 'specialise' in the area they needed help with, and I was able to undo the damage that firm had done. At the end of the engagement the client asked me to take on a permanent advisory role for one day a month, at my full daily rate.

I was sorely tempted.   That one day a month alone would have earned me enough to meet my lifestyle needs, but I had to turn the offer down. I was about to start a very full-time six-month engagement and it would have been very difficult for me to take time out for that one day a month, probably at my own expense. But once you start to build client relationships be alive to opportunities like this; a client that doesn't need you around full-time can sometimes be very receptive to arrangements where you commit to a certain number of days in a given period.

Contracting other people

It may be that as an interim manager you will find yourself with an opportunity to sell other interims to your client. This can happen because the client will simply ask you if you know someone, or because you are more proactive and suggest to the client that another person is required to solve a particular problem.

You need to be very careful when this kind of situation arises.

The easiest way to achieve the desired objective is to put the client in touch with a suitable candidate and leave them to contract between themselves.   You should ensure that the person you are recommending is suitable; just because they are a chum of yours doesn't necessarily mean they're suitable. Even where you are confident about the interim's suitability you should make it clear to the client that they (the client) should satisfy themselves as to the interim's suitability and that you cannot be held responsible if he or she doesn't work out.   Of course, even if you do make this clear to the client and the interim doesn't work out, you are not going to look good. The client might not be able to make you legally responsible for his or her failure but your reputation will be damaged. In my view it's a lot of responsibility for no reward.

Another way is to suggest to the client that you sub-contract the new interim and charge the client for his or her services. It is normal in this situation to take a margin. Even if the client is prepared to permit this (and not surprisingly many clients feel uncomfortable to say the least about their interims making a profit by selling other interims) you need to be absolutely sure that the interim you are now going to be responsible for is suitable, and that the time you are going to spend ensuring that he or she does good work is not going to distract you from achieving your own objectives. I've never done this and wouldn't feel comfortable doing so.

Another option is to allow the new interim to contract direct to the client, and to agree with him or her (the new interim) a fee arrangement between the two of you as recompense to you for the introduction and the risk you are taking on. This is normally a proportion of the fee he charges the client; 20% is the usual rate charged by agencies. It is up to you whether you declare this arrangement to your client but again it is unlikely that the client is going to be terribly happy about it. Perhaps the problem is that as an interim you are supposed to have your client's best interests at heart, and that by making a profit at the expense of the client you are betraying the client's trust?

Where you have been introduced to the client via an agency any introductions of new interims by you will normally need to be with the agency's agreement, who will usually prefer to contract the new interim themselves and take a margin. Whether they share some of this margin with you will depend on what you manage to negotiate but my advice in this situation is to insist upon it, or suggest to the agency that they find their own candidates.

All in all, it's dangerous territory. Tread carefully.

As the best in the business (and I have already said that if you are not the best in the business you should not be attempting to carve out a career as an interim) you are of course an expert at what you do and what you know. As a successful interim you will have under your belt prime evidence of recent and relevant experience, and your expertise may be valuable in a court case or tribunal. Expert witness work is in my experience fascinating and remunerative, if sometimes tedious in the extreme; hours in draughty corridors outside court rooms waiting to be called (but each hour billed at my maximum fee rate, which sugars the pill somewhat). This is not a book on how to be an expert witness (there are other books you can read on this) and I don't claim to be an expert on expert witnessing but I can give you some idea of how to find this kind of work:

- Include the words "expert witness" in your website, LinkedIn profile and CV so that any word-search will pick it up. Even if you have never done any such work there is no reason why you should not indicate your willingness to be considered;

- Whenever you can in your working life, develop relationships with law firms that you find yourself working alongside, and make sure they know just what an expert you are – and in what fields. Buy them lunch, a drink or even just coffee, drop them an email on some pretext or other every now and then, so that they will know where to find you when the opportunity arises;

- Milk any relationship you have with the bigger consultancy firms. They are often involved in large legal or tribunal cases but frequently find themselves unable to act as expert witness because they are "conflicted out"; they have a pre-existing relationship with one of the sides in the case. Such firms are often on the look-out for independents who are prepared to provide the court or tribunal with an opinion.

I have found expert witness work via all three of these routes and the work it has brought me has undoubtedly been the most fascinating of my career. I wish I could find more of it but I suppose that if it started getting in the way of my interim career there might come a point at which I could no longer claim to be an expert, my relevant experience would not necessarily be recent, and my recent experience might not necessarily be relevant. So it is just as well that I only get such work every now and then to brighten up my career, and even then I have found that expert witness work can get in the way of my interim assignments. The last thing a client wants to hear is that you are forced to take time out from solving his problems in order to help another firm sue someone (or defend a suit).

When you are offered expert witness work try to ascertain the extent of your anticipated involvement. How often will you be required to attend meetings and for how long? When is the case scheduled to appear before the Court or tribunal? How long will you be expected to attend? Having said this my experience is that a lot of my involvement as an expert witness has involved hours many poring over exhibits and making notes; work I can do perfectly well at home in the evening and at weekends without impacting on my interim commitments. My pension fund hasn't suffered at all by this.

Non-Executive Directorships

A non-executive directorship (a.k.a. an independent directorship) can fit very nicely into an interim management career; the skills, knowledge and experience required for both roles are complementary. Both roles require someone with credibility and authority with an independent and enquiring mind, a methodical approach to analysis, excellent questioning skills, highly tuned political antennae, and of course an ability to build strong relationships at the most senior level within an organisation.

There is a school of thought that the risks attached to being a Non-Executive Director just aren't worth the candle. As a NED one is required to assume responsibility for a firm where the decisions are made by the executives over whom you have no control, and you (the

NED) usually only get to hear about those decisions in hindsight every quarter, and even then you get the executive's version of events, supported by their data, their analysis and their justification.[9] And if the executives do make the wrong decision you, the poor NED, are equally as liable as the executives for any damage those decisions may have done. Is the quarterly Board attendance fee really worth that risk?

I am sympathetic to this view to some extent, and if you are ever offered an opportunity to become a NED you should of course consider the risks carefully. I'm afraid I can't in this book cover this ground with anything like adequacy; if you get offered a non-executive directorship you should take care, and seek advice.

I have occasionally been offered non-executive directorships and turned them down because they were not right for a number of reasons, and because of the hassle of turning up every quarter to a Board meeting, to say nothing of the time that would be required reading Board papers, the Audit Committee attendances, the special meetings, etc. It was just not worth the distraction from my other commitments. My attitude may well change in the future, if I am ever again offered an opportunity.

---

[9] You think this is a jaundiced view? As a senior executive can you honestly say that you have never found yourself employing spin, guile and 'economy with the truth' to persuade a recalcitrant and reactionary Board to agree to your proposals? Do you think that when you are on the other side of the table the world will somehow be different?

Andrew Gordon's Code of Ethics

These five very simple principles are something I have tried to live by in my interim career. They have stood me in good stead and I recommend them to you[10].

1. **If It Isn't Broken, Don't Fix It:** As an interim I try to focus on the important stuff where I can make a difference. I don't try to make changes just because I prefer things done "my way". In an interim assignment there is more than enough to do fixing the things that are genuinely broken. Work with the materials you have, and where you can build on what you inherited rather than try to dismantle and re-build it. There are times when a complete reconstruction is unavoidable but in my experience these are rare.

2. **Don't Shirk the Difficult Stuff**: It is very easy as an interim to avoid things that are in the 'too difficult' box and to concentrate instead on the easy wins that will make you look like you are achieving something. You should not avoid tackling the big issues if they need tackling, even where this will make your life harder. You are a professional, after all. But at the same time, be realistic: You have only a few months to solve problems and you need to ensure that whatever objectives you set yourself and agree with your client are going to be achievable in that time frame. Pushing boulders halfway up a hill isn't going to do anyone any good.

---

[10] The Institute of Interim Management has its own Code. It's rather longer than mine but perfectly sound: *https://iim.org.uk/wp-content/uploads/2016/06/code-of-conduct-1.pdf*

3. **Strive For Permanent Solutions:** As an interim I try to help the client arrive at a long-lasting solution to their challenges, as soon as practicably achievable. I want to solve the problem in a way that ensures that if it arises again my support will not be needed because the client's own staff will be able to deal with it. I therefore do whatever I can to achieve the desired results using the client's own resources, and to achieve a successful handover.

4. **Never Undermine the Position of a Colleague, or Criticise Your Predecessor:** If management asks me to give a critique of an individual's performance I am of course happy to do so in a fair and open manner. I do not do so by commenting on an individual's performance behind his back. If someone has left the organisation there is normally no need for me to comment on his performance at all. If I find issues that my predecessor has left behind I solve them without drawing unnecessary attention to them. One can never really know what pressures and constraints your predecessor was working under, so don't judge. It won't make you any friends if you do.

5. **Do Not Encourage Colleagues to Consider Leaving Their Current Employer**, either during or after your assignment (unless of course, it is with your client's blessing as part of a cost-reduction campaign). That is simply not what your client wants or needs; it would be nothing short of an act of betrayal.

Some of these principles, but particularly the first two, may not seem at first to have any connection with a code of ethics. But my experience as a young management consultant was that we were strongly encouraged, once we had shouldered open the client's door and infiltrated his organisation, to look for other opportunities to 'help' the client, and on the back of that to sell other consultancy work, earning ourselves big bonuses if we were successful. Often of course these opportunities were genuine and the sales made honestly but I have to say that sometimes it seemed to me that we were identifying non-existent problems, or focusing on problems that were lucrative (for us, not for the client!) to fix, rather than work on the more urgent and pressing challenges that could be fixed swiftly and cheaply. (A problem that required lots of junior, newly-qualified accountant to resolve would have my consultancy bosses positively drooling; we had to find something for the kiddiewinks to do, after all.)

And before you think I am setting myself up as a paragon of interim virtue let me admit that I have broken Principle 4, and paid dearly for doing so. It was an important lesson. Just because I think someone is an incompetent, devious, bullying, untrustworthy idiot (which he certainly was) it does not give me the right to describe him as such when asked, however informally, for my professional opinion. A professional opinion should be just that; professional. And it's only my opinion, which is fallible.

I have also broken Principle 5 but in my defence it was at the behest of the client who was very keen to solve a problem caused by an individual who had been wrongly recruited to a role he (the individual) could not fulfil. The organisation was suffering from his inability to meet the requirements of the role, and the individual was suffering from stress for the same reason. It was best for all concerned that he moved to another organisation and role where his talents were a better match. I achieved this, and at the time of writing he is still working for his new employer who is delighted with his services. He's happy too. This is the kind of situation where I can sometimes feel good about what I do, but they're rare.

And finally...

As an interim I occupy the gaps, the interstices of life. I act as a bridge between a predecessor's leaving party and his permanent successor's first day. I make maternity and paternity periods possible. I fill the gap between an organisation's ambition and its capability, and meet shortfalls in resources. I create a vital link between junior staff and senior management. I help my clients wallpaper over cracks and paint over blemishes. I hide other people's mistakes, solve other people's problems, and push forward other people's careers.

These gaps can sometimes prove to be very dull, nothing more than ways to make a good living with no real job satisfaction. But they can also be fascinating; interims can find themselves exploring all sorts of organisational nooks and crannies. It is a life that brings a philosophy of its own; I find myself, as each assignment draws to a close, wondering: "So, what next? - where are the cards going to fall this time?" My interim career has taught me that one can find job satisfaction in even the most unlikely roles; any job, if approached with a positive curiosity, can yield its rewards. The important thing is to maintain that positive attitude, to be prepared to take roles that are outside your comfort zone, or are not necessarily conducive or well-paid. To some extent you have to be prepared to take life as it comes, to go with the flow and not worry too much about where it might take you. It is a kind of freedom that can be very liberating, although for many quite frightening. If you have always enjoyed planning your career, then interim management is not for you. As an interim I accept that my career has in that sense reached a dead end; I will never rise higher up the organisational hierarchy than I am now, and I have no wish to do so.

So, you think you can achieve success as an interim manager? Then come on in - the water's lovely! But remember; no one goes to their grave wishing they'd spent more time at the office. For me, life as an interim is about being able to balance my need to make a living with my preference for doing what I want to do. I have learned to say "No".

If this book encourages you to jump in, let me know how you get on. I wish you all the luck in the world!

Best wishes

Andrew Gordon

Case Studies

What follows are two case studies from my career which, I hope, explain how I learned the lessons that I am now sharing with you, and put those lessons into the context of a real-life assignment. They are not MBA-type case studies, or the kind of case studies you will find on the interim management websites full of guff about how Mr Super Interim Manager achieved a squillion dollar increase in profits whilst simultaneously improving customer satisfaction and reducing costs, blah, blah. What I give you here is my honest account of what I was asked to do by my client, what I then decided to do (and I hope by now you will have learned that these are rarely the same thing) and how I actually went about it.

I have chosen two assignments from my career; one that went well, and one that went badly. In order to spare my former clients' blushes, and to keep their organisations' lawyers at bay, I have had to change some of the characters, and the locations of the assignments, and some of the circumstance attached to the assignments but please be assured that the achievements I describe, and the mistakes I own up to, are cringingly real.

Case Study 1

The challenge

I was asked by a large foreign-owned multi-media publisher to take charge of a 60-strong Internal Audit department following the departure "by mutual consent" of my predecessor. This assignment was early on in my interim career and my brief was to simply act as caretaker until my successor could be found. The organisation had already appointed a head-hunter to find my successor "at any cost", and I was given my predecessor's job description which contained the kind of instructions that job descriptions normally contain; the usual exhortations to 'do good' but with nothing specific in terms of what 'good' might look like.

I was naïve in those days, and very happy to have been contacted out of the blue by this relatively prestigious firm and asked to take on the role, particularly as they didn't seem too fussy about the fee rate I quoted. I soon learned that they were desperate, and very glad to find someone able and willing to do it, and in fact in my career since then I have learned that normally when I am approached directly by a firm for an interim role I am probably the only realistic candidate currently available. So I did not take the time before signing the contract to get my client - the lady who was to become my client boss - to articulate what the main problems were and what she expected me to do about them.

My first few days

So I arrived bright and early on the Monday morning, terribly eager to impress, in a new suit and shirt. I was neat, clean-shaven and sober and I didn't care who knew it.[11] My predecessor had left several weeks before my arrival and so I had no chance to quiz him on what the issues might be. My boss, a frighteningly clever, expensively dressed and utterly charming Jewish lady of a certain age met me at 9am and gave me a more candid briefing than she had been prepared to give me during our interview: I had inherited, apparently, a department full of 'no-hopers' and 'schmucks' whom she expected would need to be replaced and/or augmented; she referred repeatedly to the need for "fresh blood". She then whisked me into a large conference room where my team had been called together to meet their new boss, thrust me into the limelight and told me to introduce myself.

Although I had not been expecting this I was able to give them ten minutes about who I was, what I was looking for, and what I hoped to give them. Because this was off-the-cuff and unprepared it actually went quite well; I engaged my audience, invited questions

---

[11] I didn't have the socks with clocks in them.

which I answered as honestly as I could, threw in a couple of jokes, and my boss was pleased. I had arrived.

I was then shown to my office; a ten foot by eight foot glass 'fish-tank' complete with a PA sitting outside to act as my gatekeeper. To my new PA's horror I immediately turned the office into a meeting room for anyone to use, and set up my desk in the middle of the open-plan floor, amongst all of my staff, where I could overhear conversations and observe work activity without making it obvious that I was doing any such thing.

I instructed my PA to book a one-hour meeting with my four direct reports, and a half-hour meeting with everyone else in my department. These meetings were conducted anywhere other than the room which had formerly been my office; in the coffee area, the local pub, any quiet area we could cadge. I was determined to ensure that the meetings were seen as informal 'getting to know you' sessions rather than formal interviews.

In the first week I also asked for - and by and large got - meetings with all of my peers within the business, to ask them what they thought of my department and what needed to be done to improve its services and its reputation.

By the end of my second week - an exhausting whirlwind ten days - I had much of the information and insight I needed to see why the department had such a bad relationship with the business, and I had a pretty good idea of what needed to be done to put it right. Needless to say, these views were at odds with what my boss thought needed to be done...

What I discovered

The department had indeed a terrible reputation within the organisation. The CEO (my boss' boss) was a large and rather imposing character, and in my first introduction to him he made it plain what he thought of the department - which wasn't much. He repeatedly accused it of being "behind the wicket" by which, it turned out, he meant that in his perception it focused on highlighting problems after they had emerged rather than assisting management in preventing them from occurring in the first place; a common criticism aimed at Internal Audit departments.

Indeed the organisation's general lack of regard for their Internal Audit function was obvious. The department had been moved to a building that was physically separate from the rest of the organisation; a down-at-heel building the other side of town that had last been decorated in the seventies and which was far too small for us. In particular I recall most vividly the orange and brown carpet, and the drinks machine that served God-awful tea and coffee (I was never quite sure which was which) and the sometimes irritating, sometimes very welcome 20-minute schlep across town to the Head Office (there were times when I was grateful for the fresh air). We were the only department - other than that other Cinderella department 'Facilities' - that had been allocated to this building; literally a case of 'out of sight, out of mind'.

My department was structured in an odd way: Out of a department of 60 I was given only four direct reports, three of whom were eye-wateringly expensive in terms of their salary and benefits and who had recently been recruited from outside the firm to their newly-recruited roles. Below these four were six 'Team Leaders', and below these were various grades of worker, some of whom reported to a Team Leader and some of whom reported to people who reported to a Team Leader. The department had four layers of management including myself!

The organisation was going through a difficult time. Within the first couple of days I realised that few of my colleagues, both inside and outside my department, seemed to see any long-term future for the business, and by quiet discussion with my boss (who had been rather coy when interviewing me for the role) and my peers I learned that the firm was probably being prepared for sale by its foreign parent, although at that time no-one was prepared to state this as a fact, for obvious commercial reasons. Certainly the political landscape seemed to be focused in that direction; the emphasis was on the almost artificial inflation of profit by the cancellation of any project that was not scheduled to deliver revenue benefit within that financial year, and cost-cutting wherever possible. This was not an organisation that was interested in investing for the future.

Morale in my department was rock-bottom. This was due to a number of factors but the most pressing was the widespread realisation that the department was unregarded, with poorly allocated roles and responsibilities, an allocation that bore no obvious connection with people's skills and interests. Many of my people wanted to leave and were keeping an eye on the jobs pages. Some were honest enough to tell me that they had already attended interviews with other organisations.

One of the reasons the department's reputation was failing was due to the weaknesses of the people within the department; the people who owned and managed the business relationship. Many of them had not been properly briefed on their roles, or given time to manage the relationship properly, or were simply unsuited to the role. The department's structure meant that the people within my department who had the relationship with the business were quite junior and in some cases were not sufficiently skilled to handle the responsibility; they simply lacked credibility. The department did not lack talent but what talent it had, had been very badly allocated.

Because the knowledge of what was going on in the business - what services the organisation needed and what my department should provide - was held at a junior level, my senior guys relied on endless internal meetings to find out what was going on, and then adding their interpretation on events, interpretation that was often very wide of the mark. And then they would give instructions to the junior guys about how to respond, which the junior guys would take with a pinch of salt... My predecessor had obviously been very fond of internal meetings; a common trait among failing managers.

A lot of the department's activity was not really audit work. The department had hitherto been used as the dustbin of the organisation and had been given tasks that the other departments simply didn't

105

want. These tasks included, for example, customer complaints handling, performing routine quality assurance work on behalf of other department heads, and some financial reporting which we were not really qualified to do and which in many cases just turned us into a conduit for information; we were adding no value to the report. In fact I quickly gained the impression that I had inherited the relics of an empire-builder; a rag-bag of tasks, responsibilities and activities loosely stuck together to justify someone's inflated salary, or sense of worth, or both.

Some of my team were, shall we say, stronger than others, and strength did not necessarily correlate with seniority. Three of my direct reports – the three expensive ones - did not justify their vast salaries, and I concluded that my predecessor had probably created their roles (and their salaries) in order to inflate his own, and cover his own weaknesses.

What I did

Over a period of time I reduced the department's head count by half, by:

a) Making my three expensive direct reports redundant. I did this within the first few weeks of my arrival, and this alone reduced my salary bill by nearly half!

b) Transferring some of my team to other departments; the departments to which we were providing services that were not related to internal audit.

c) With my boss' blessing, and with the assistance of Human Resources department, helping some people who were unhappy or under-utilised move to other organisations. This meant losing some of my better people but I would rather help a strong person find a new employer than make a weaker person redundant.

I then restructured the department so that I had eight direct reports; the 'engine-room'. To fill these posts I selected eight individuals who had the knowledge of the business and the skills to manage the relationship, thereby putting myself in complete command of how the department ran, and in touch with what was going on in the organisation and what we needed to do to respond to its needs.

These changes reduced the management levels within the department to three; each of my eight reports managed a small team, all of whom reported to one of the eight. This allowed me to promote some of the stronger people whose talents had up to then been hidden within a large and badly-run department.

With my new team structure I re-allocated objectives and tasks based on people's skills and inclinations. I did this by negotiation; everyone was given an opportunity to apply for roles and activities, and with some horse-trading I found that jobs fell to the people most suited to them. The objectives I set the teams were aligned to the business's own structure; each major function and project within the firm was allocated a representative from Internal Audit (we called this "shadowing"). I personally briefed my guys on what was expected of the role. I also introduced each of my representatives to the part of the business they were shadowing, explained what their role was to the head of the relevant department or project, and asked for feedback. I kept in touch with every one of the heads of department or project to ensure that my people were giving them what they needed.

Finally, I took the youngest and cheapest of the four direct reports originally allocated to me and started to groom him as my successor. He was in any case by far the most talented of the original four, and the most highly-regarded within and without the department. It was a joy to see him grow into the role; all he had needed was an opportunity, and I gave it him in spades. He was well-liked, and having worked within the organisation since leaving college in a variety of roles he had strong business knowledge and strong internal relationships. The news that he was being developed as my successor was so warmly received that my kudos soared; I was seen as the good guy looking out for the people to whom the business owed a great deal. In fact my decision to appoint him was one of the easiest decisions I have ever made.

My boss, who was close to retirement and looking for an easy life, was scared by some of the decisions I made regarding the down-sizing of the department. In the early stage of my assignment I did not take as much time as required to keep her comfortable with what was going on. As soon as I realised this I insisted upon weekly half-hour sessions with her, and I told her PA firmly that these meetings were sacrosanct. She soon came to rely on those meetings for other reasons and we developed an excellent working relationship, to the extent that when she surprised me by declining an opportunity to take early retirement and instead take on a big role at another firm I was the first person she called for when she got there. Which was nice...

The outcome

The department was able to re-build its relationship with the business by fielding skilled people with credibility and business acumen. Our reputation soared as we started to add value to meetings and projects, to the extent that we began to be called in to any new project to provide advice, and I was astonished at how quickly this happened. (I was later told by my boss that removing the three really expensive guys had sent an early, loud and very welcome signal to the business that things were changing; the three were not generally liked.)

Moral within the department went sky-high as those with talent suddenly found themselves in the spotlight and given an opportunity to prove themselves. Some people who deserved it - and who were widely recognised as deserving it - were promoted. This was despite the fact that I was at the same time making redundancies. It could have been very easy for me to fall into the trap of being seen as the 'hatchet man' but I was able to reduce headcount by half, and my salary bill by two-thirds, with only three compulsory redundancies; the three expensive direct reports that no-one in the department shed a tear over; they were seen by everyone as over-paid.

We started doing the work an Internal Audit department is supposed to do and is qualified to do, and became recognised as a business enabler.

We reduced our internal departmental meetings to once a week, each taking no more than one hour. We suddenly had a lot more time to do what we were supposed to do; provide a service to our internal customers.

I found a worthy successor and saved my client the head-hunter's fee.

The final accolade came when the CEO instructed my boss to bring us into the main head office building, and we were given a spacious, newly-decorated suite right next to his office (with a lovely new blue carpet). He called me and my successor - my successor had by then been announced and I was providing him with handover support - into his office and gave us the task of assisting with the next big project; preparing the business for sale and managing the 'due diligence' process.

The lessons

All in all it was a gruelling but very successful nine months, and one which, looking back, set me on the road to becoming an interim. I had had previous interim assignments but this was the first in which I ignored my client's request to simply act as caretaker and instead set myself a series of challenges based on my own reading of the organisation's situation and its needs. I learned a huge amount; it was also the first time I had managed a department of that size and the first time I had made people redundant. I look back on my nine months spent in that organisation as the real start of my interim career and the lessons I learned there have stood me in good stead. This book is based on many of them. I make no apology for repeating them here:

It is vital that you take the opportunity, when negotiating a new interim role, to get your potential boss to explain the situation you are being asked to take ownership of, and what he expects you to do about them. I failed to do this, and although I quickly recovered the situation it was an early wobble I could have done without. Some of my changes surprised her, and because I drifted so far away from her original instruction to "just mind the shop" it could have made our lives difficult. That it didn't is because I got it right; if I had got anything wrong I would have been in grave difficulty.

When you take on a new department be prepared to introduce yourself to them as a group. Off-the-cuff presentations are much better for being prepared! - but do make it look like it is genuinely off-the-cuff; slide shows are not acceptable.

Take time to meet *everyone* on a one-to-one basis, both within and without your department. What they tell you will be hugely valuable; even if you don't agree with what is said you will at least know what's on their mind. Remember that perception is the only reality; you may disagree with what you are being told but what that person sees as the truth is just as important as what you think is truth, and maybe even more so. So shut up and listen. You will have time to talk later, when you properly understand the situation. Expect some kite-flying and political agendas but at least it's nice to know what the kites and agendas are so that you can recognise them when you next see them. They will probably become old friends, and who knows, they may even turn out to be valid.

Take people as you find them. I had been told by my boss that my department was full of 'shmucks' and 'no-hopers' but this was far from the case; they had simply been inappropriately allocated to tasks, and poorly trained and supported. I was delighted at how quickly the natural talent of some of my team came to the fore when they were given an opportunity to show what they could do. When I am told that I am taking on people who need to be replaced I have invariably (and there really has been no exception to this rule) found that with the right training, support, encouragement and above all recognition I have been perfectly content to work with what I have been given. Teams are only as strong as their leader, and it is actually very difficult to find good new people (and very time consuming - time you are unlikely to have as an interim).

I tend now to assume that in any large organisation my successor is probably already employed by the firm; all I need to do is find him and give him the skills and confidence he needs. This may not prove to be true but it is still the right attitude to take. Automatically reaching for a head-hunter is a lazy solution; it acknowledges that you have not arranged a succession plan, or bothered to develop someone in readiness. The benefits of appointing an internal candidate are so great that you really do need to be sure you have no-one even remotely suitable before you look for external candidates.

Keep your boss close to you. A weekly meeting - even for just 20 minutes - is hugely valuable, so that you can explain what you are doing and ensure he is comfortable with that, and it gives you an opportunity to test your ideas out in a relatively safe environment. My boss was the model of decorum and unfailingly polite but she was not slow in telling me when she thought I was going out on a limb. Sometimes I persuaded her otherwise, and sometimes I was grateful for the friendly warning.

Read the political environment. In this case I recognised that the department was seen, with some justification, as a bloated dysfunctional behemoth that was operating to an agenda that was not what the organisation needed. In a firm that was preparing itself for sale we needed to concentrate on helping the business reduce costs, maximise revenue, and prepare for the rigour of sales-side due diligence, whilst at the same time reducing our own departmental budget. I dismantled the empire my failed predecessor had built up, and re-focused it on what the business really wanted, much to everyone's relief. I had been given my boss' sanction to replace my team with 'new blood' and to spend a lot of money doing so - but I chose a different path, and it worked.

As an interim I have often found myself working for an organisation that is being prepared for sale, or merger, or closure, or some other major event. This is not surprising; organisations facing major and potentially unhappy sea changes are prone to suddenly losing senior managers and are inclined to be short-termist; ideal conditions for the immediate, short-term solution of an interim. If you are going to be successful as an interim in the private sector you need to learn the realities of life in an organisation that is in this situation, and respond to them.

Case Study 2

The challenge

I was contacted by an agency and asked to meet a well-know UK high street bank that was looking for someone to establish a brand new Risk & Compliance Monitoring department. At the time I was just recovering from a very intensive six months working for another bank in Scotland and I was not inclined to work for another. In fact I have subsequently promised myself that hell will freeze over before I work for another UK retail bank, and perhaps this Case Study will explain why...

When I met the client - the man who was to be my boss - I was quite impressed. He was a young (well, younger than me) South African who had himself been an interim for the bank but who had accepted a permanent role. He was clearly bright, and brought a refreshingly un-stuffy (dare I say it un-British) approach to the challenges the bank was having in managing its risks, and the conversation we had around how to approach the task was one of mutual understanding and agreement.

The conversation took a slightly colder turn when it came to my fees. I quoted a rate which was £200 a day more than the absolute top rate he was "authorised" to offer. I declined to reduce my rate, and our meeting ended on this slightly sour note. I left the bank's glamorous London head office doubting that I would be hearing from them again. In fact, I received a call the next day asking when I could start.

My first few days

My first task was to recruit a new department of around 25 people. Some were already allocated to me; a rag-bag collection of refugees from other departments that were being wound up, or people that were surplus to requirements, and even some former (failed) branch managers who had chosen my department as an alternative to redundancy or early retirement. I learned that the bank was undergoing one of its regular "re-organisations", a process that seemed to involve cutting people adrift from their current role and seeing where they washed up.

I was allowed to supplement this initial allocation with my own choice of individuals - so long as they were internal candidates selected from those who had been given redundancy notices.

It was not an auspicious start, to say the least. I found myself the manager of a 25-strong department made up of people with little or no relevant skills, and with little enthusiasm for the roles in which they found themselves. Many had applied for a role in my department as their second or even third choice. Some of them were honest enough to tell me that they had accepted the role simply as a way of avoiding redundancy, and that as soon as they found a more conducive role they would be leaving. One of them was petulant to the point of hostility.

What I did:

With a heavy heart I called them together to our first meeting, which took place in one of the bank's more dreary administration centres in a business park on the outskirts of a town in the Midlands. I had rehearsed my speech, and believe me, Shakespeare's Henry V presented a less compelling argument for commitment to the task than I did that day.

I had done my homework. I gave an overview of the bank's difficulties and challenges with regard to risk management, difficulties that had not been overlooked by its regulator. I explained to them the brief we (note that at no time did I say "I) had been given. I showed how a good Risk and Compliance Monitoring function fitted into a modern, well-run bank, and the difference it can make to the bank's treatment of its customers and to its long-term commercial success. I talked about my experiences in other banks (I had the advantage of having worked for two of the bank's closest

114

competitors) and I emphasised the value of the opportunity that was being put their way; an opportunity to show the bank their mettle "for there is none of you so mean and base, that hath not noble lustre in your eyes". (Okay, I didn't quite put it like that, but you get the picture.)

It worked! Sinews visibly stiffened, blood was summoned, and teeth were set. People began to share their experiences of just how badly managed the bank was. Evidence was presented of risks that had been realised because senior management were ignorant of them, or complacent, or had under-estimated their potential impact. We talked about the impact of those risks on the poor customer, on staff, and on profits. One of the advantages of such a disparate set of people was the huge wealth of experiences they brought with them; we estimated that in that meeting alone we had over 350 years of experience of working for the bank. One of my younger and more enthusiastic colleagues began to write on a flip-chart.

The result

That meeting became something of a minor legend in the short history of the department. It was the start of the department as a department, and from the flip-charts that were drawn up that day a detailed plan was developed which identified the key risks facing the bank, and people volunteered to do further work to properly understand, measure and address each risk.

I interviewed and allocated team leaders to run review teams. With the assistance of a friend of mine borrowed from an external consultancy firm we developed and ran a series of courses that gave the team the skills they needed, including interviewing skills, audit and investigation skills, and report-writing and professional presentation skills. (This was the only external assistance I was allowed, although to be honest I am not sure I would have asked for more, even if it had been available.)

Some of the key risks we identified were of course highly sensitive to the bank's commercial viability and its relationship with the

115

regulator, and it put huge pressure on me to run a department which attempted to flush out those risks, and force management to address them, with such an inexperienced team. But I was determined to show what could be done, and to capitalise on the enthusiasm I had tapped into. It had all seemed to come together very well, and gave me huge confidence in my ability to manage. I gave my team their head, and with their newly developed investigation, analysis and reporting skills, they began to make themselves known. They visited branches and discovered selling practices that were bordering on fraudulent. They reviewed head office functions and identified major system flaws and errors. They talked to customers and gained unique insights into the way the bank treated (or mistreated) them. Our findings were distilled into compelling reports that were difficult to argue with. One of our findings was so significant that the bank was forced to report the situation to the regulator and undertake extensive remedial action.

I can't tell you what these findings were, I'm afraid, because the bank has some very expensive and aggressive lawyers. I should know; I met them all during meetings in which we discussed, in all earnestness, how to pull the wool over the regulator's eyes. (This is in fact ludicrously easy, and it doesn't take a £500 per hour lawyer to work it out.)

Well, you've probably guessed it. My department's effectiveness and energy is exactly what the bank did not want. Our risk identification had touched some raw nerves, and exposed too many skeletons. Our pithy, factual reports began to disappear into a political quicksand that Sir Humphrey Appleby (the senior civil servant in the BBC hit comedy "Yes, Minister") would have been proud of. The bank's complex, inter-connected and labyrinthine system of protocols, sacred cows and shibboleths were under threat, to say nothing of its profits and share price, and that was just unacceptable.

The spineless venality of the UK's big retail banks really was then breathtaking. I can only conclude that this is why these organisations have a tradition of encouraging and rewarding long service. Staff members who are in all other respects decent people - loving partners to their spouses, decent parents, concerned about the environment, generous to charities, etc - need to become inured, I might even say brainwashed, into accepting that when they cross the threshold of their workplace they have the right, if not the duty, to treat the customer as a gullible fool from whom they must extract as much money as possible, regardless of the customer's needs or wants. For a new employee (or interim) who steps into their world from outside, it is just astounding. It reminds me of those appalling experiments about prison camp guards and the attitude they inevitably develop towards their prisoners.

My weekly meetings with my boss became more and more difficult as he tried to force me to bury the findings that my team were unearthing, despite my assurances that the risks were manageable. He was a very political animal. For example, I got into trouble for discussing one of the risks over an informal lunch with my boss' boss without first agreeing the lunch's agenda with him. As my team's enthusiasm rose by leaps and bounds, mine plumbed new depths.

The point at which I was asked to help the bank be more than just a little devious with its regulator was the point at which I began to make urgent arrangements for my departure. Fortunately the bank had already identified a potential successor; a very capable acquaintance of mine who had recently been made redundant and was more prepared to navigate the political seas that existed within the bank. I was candid with her and explained the difficulties I had experienced, but she was anxious to find well-paid work, and the role fitted her child-care requirements perfectly. It was close to her home, and like most modern organisations the bank was willing to accept flexible, part-time working arrangements. She took the role, and I left just before the end of my six-month contractual period.

I have never been happier to leave an organisation in my life, and it is the only time in my interim career that I have left an assignment before the end of the planned contractual period. My team members gave me a tremendous send-off, and I have kept in touch with many of them. Some of them had become so enthused with their new role that it became the start of new careers for them, both within the bank and for other organisations.

My boss did not bother to say thank you for my efforts. Again, this is the only time this has ever happened.

Some time after I left the department was largely disbanded; a victim of another of the bank's 'reorganisations'. My boss was also promoted to a bigger role within the bank. I follow his career with interest. I see him on television occasionally, normally when another banking scandal has become headline news, explaining why his bank would never stoop to such practices. He will go far.

The lessons

Well, they are probably obvious to you, Dear Reader. Perhaps you think that they are so obvious that you are confident that you will be able to avoid making such blundering mistakes yourself? I hope you are right.

If you are asked to establish a brand new department, make sure you understand how the members of the department are to be recruited. Confirm that you will have a realistic budget for training, and for any other external help that you might need.

If you are asked to set up a new department that by its nature is one which is expected to challenge the organisation, don't expect to be thanked for achieving this. Examples of such departments are Internal Audit and any of its comparable internal review departments, and I would also include Compliance, Quality Assurance, Risk Management, Human Resources, and Health & Safety. My cynical view is that these departments only last when they are not *too* successful, so maybe they suit the interim manager who is more prepared to play the politically astute game - or at the very least, the assignment is more likely to run its full course.

Never write off the team you have been given. Get their enthusiasm, and you will discover just what talent you have at your disposal. There may be gaps in their skills but skills can be taught. This has been an attitude I have taken into every one of my interim assignments and it has never let me down. And you don't need to be Henry V to engage enthusiasm. You just need to be honest about the challenges, genuinely committed to the task in hand, and willing to ask for their help.

In fact I am not sure that the concept of 'talent' is really relevant in most working environments. There are very few career choices that depend for success on some God-given ability. The climb up the greasy pole to all but the very senior levels is achieved by enthusiasm, application, hard work, commonsense, and a few tricks that involve getting the best out of the people you meet. These are attitudes, and the behaviours - the skills - that stem from these attitudes, that are sometimes innate but can also be learned. The lessons are not even difficult. So we can all become 'talented', if we want to be. It just takes a little discipline, and a willingness to learn and adapt ourselves to the demands of whatever working environment we find ourselves. And in case you were wondering, the journey up the last few feet of the greasy pole demands two other things: Luck, and a preparedness to shove your competitors off the pole.

If you are asked to work for a British retail bank be very careful about the role you are asked to take on. If it is for one of the challenge departments described above, be prepared to play the political game, and console yourself with the money they will throw at you. Pride and professional integrity have their place but there are times when they will constrain your interim career. Keep reminding yourself; you are in this game to make money, not to change the world. By all means do what you can to put things right but remember that that is not what the client is paying you for. Stating on your CV that "I made the world a slightly better place" is unlikely to impress future clients, even though in life that is all one can ever really hope for.

Useful contacts

Interim Management Association
Website: http://www.interimmanagement.uk.com/

Institute of Interim Management
Website: http://www.iim.org/

People Management **online: interim employment section**
Website: http://www.peoplemanagement.co.uk/pm/sections/interim
employment/

Further reading

CLUTTERBUCK, D. *and* **DEARLOVE, D.** *The interim manager: a new career model for the experienced manager.* London, Financial Times Pitman Publishing, 1998.
ISBN 0273632930

HILL, Julie. *Interim executive management.* London, Caspian, 2002. (Business guide).
ISBN 1901844331

www.ingramcontent.com/pod-product-compliance
Lightning Source LLC
Chambersburg PA
CBHW070031210526

45170CB00012B/532

* 9 7 8 0 2 4 4 6 4 4 4 3 7 *